TABLE OF CONTENTS

INTRODUCTION

At its core, content marketing is about creating and sharing valuable, relevant, and consistent content to attract and engage a clearly defined audience. Unlike traditional advertising methods that push messages out to consumers, content marketing focuses on providing useful information that pulls people in, fostering trust and building lasting relationships.

High-quality content positions your brand as an authority in your industry. By consistently delivering insightful and valuable information, you demonstrate your expertise, which helps to establish credibility and trust with your audience. When customers see your brand as a reliable source of information, they are more likely to choose your products or services over competitors.

Engaging content captivates your audience and encourages them to interact with your brand. Content is everywhere around you. Whether it is blog posts, social media updates, videos, or newsletters, content provides multiple touchpoints for connecting with customers. These interactions help to build a community around your brand, fostering loyalty and advocacy. Loyal customers are not only more likely to make repeat purchases but also to recommend your brand to others, amplifying your reach organically.

Search engines prioritize high-quality, relevant content, making content marketing a critical component of search engine optimization (SEO). By regularly publishing well-crafted content that addresses the needs and interests of your target audience, you improve your chances of ranking higher in search engine results. This increased visibility drives organic traffic to your website, reducing your reliance on paid advertising and providing a steady stream of potential customers.

INTRODUCTION

Content plays a crucial role at every stage of the buyer's journey, from awareness to consideration to decision. Informative blog posts and articles can attract potential customers at the awareness stage, educational videos and case studies can help them evaluate their options during the consideration stage, and detailed product guides and testimonials can influence their decision. By mapping your content to the buyer's journey, you ensure that you are meeting your audience's needs at each step, guiding them smoothly towards conversion.

Compelling content not only attracts and engages your audience but also drives conversions. Effective content marketing addresses the pain points and challenges of your target audience, providing them with solutions that lead to action. Whether it's signing up for a newsletter, downloading a resource, or making a purchase, strategically crafted content can significantly enhance your conversion rates.

As consumer behavior evolves, so too must your marketing strategies. Today's consumers are more informed and discerning than ever before, often conducting extensive research before making purchasing decisions. They seek out brands that provide value and resonate with their needs and interests. Content marketing allows you to adapt to these changes by offering personalized, relevant content that meets the expectations of modern consumers.

In a landscape that is constantly evolving, the need for quality content remains constant. Its importance cannot be overstated, as it forms the foundation upon which all other marketing efforts are built.

CHAPTER 1

Understanding Content Marketing

DEFINITION AND IMPORTANCE

Content marketing is a strategic marketing approach focused on creating, distributing, and promoting valuable, relevant, and consistent content to attract and retain a clearly defined audience. The ultimate goal is to drive profitable customer action by providing information that educates, entertains, or inspires your audience, rather than directly promoting your products or services. This method relies on building trust and authority with your audience, fostering long-term relationships that lead to customer loyalty and increased sales.

Key Elements of Content Marketing:

- **Value:** The content should provide real value to the audience, addressing their needs, challenges, or interests.

- **Relevance:** The content must be relevant to the target audience, aligning with their interests and the stage they are at in the buyer's journey.

- **Consistency:** Regularly publishing content helps maintain engagement and keeps the audience connected to the brand.

- **Distribution:** Effective content marketing involves distributing content through the right channels to reach the intended audience.

- **Promotion:** Amplifying content through various means such as social media, email marketing, and SEO ensures it reaches a wider audience.

Importance of Content Marketing:

Building Brand Awareness and Authority: Content marketing helps in establishing your brand as a thought leader in your industry. By consistently publishing insightful and authoritative content, you position your brand as an expert, which helps build credibility and trust among your audience. When consumers see your brand as a knowledgeable resource, they are more likely to engage with your products or services.

Enhancing Customer Engagement and Retention: Engaging content fosters interaction and connection with your audience. It provides multiple touchpoints for engagement, whether through blog posts, social media interactions, videos, or newsletters. Consistent engagement keeps your audience interested and invested in your brand, leading to higher customer retention rates and brand loyalty.

Supporting SEO and Driving Organic Traffic: Quality content is a critical factor in search engine optimization (SEO). Search engines prioritize websites that regularly publish relevant, high-quality content. By creating content that addresses the queries and interests of your target audience, you improve your chances of ranking higher in search engine results pages (SERPs). Higher rankings lead to increased organic traffic to your website, reducing the need for paid advertising and providing a sustainable source of potential customers.

Guiding the Customer Journey: Content marketing is essential at every stage of the customer journey—from awareness to consideration to decision. At the awareness stage, informative blog posts and articles can attract potential customers. During the consideration stage, educational videos and case studies help them evaluate their options. Finally, detailed product guides and testimonials can influence their decision-making process. By mapping content to the buyer's journey, you ensure that you are addressing the needs of your audience at each step, guiding them towards conversion.

Increasing Conversion Rates: Well-crafted content addresses the pain points and challenges of your target audience, offering solutions that lead to action. Effective content marketing includes clear calls-to-action (CTAs) that guide your audience towards desired outcomes, such as signing up for a newsletter, downloading a resource, or making a purchase. By providing valuable information and guiding your audience through the decision-making process, content marketing can significantly enhance your conversion rates.

Adaptability to Changing Consumer Behavior: As consumer behavior evolves, content marketing allows brands to stay relevant by providing personalized and relevant content that meets the expectations of modern consumers. Today's consumers are more informed and conduct extensive research before making purchasing decisions. Content marketing enables you to meet these needs by delivering the right information at the right time, fostering trust and engagement.

Cost-Effectiveness: Compared to traditional marketing methods, content marketing is often more cost-effective. While it requires an investment of time and resources, the long-term benefits of building a loyal audience and generating organic traffic can outweigh the costs. Additionally, content can be repurposed and reused across various platforms, maximizing its value and reach.

KEY BENEFITS FOR BUSINESSES

1. Increased Brand Visibility and Awareness

Creating and distributing high-quality content helps businesses increase their visibility in the digital space. When potential customers search for information related to your industry, well-optimized content can rank higher in search engine results pages (SERPs), making it easier for people to find your brand. Consistent content publication keeps your brand top-of-mind and establishes a strong online presence.

2. Building and Establishing Authority

By sharing valuable and insightful content, businesses can position themselves as thought leaders and experts in their industry. This authority is built over time as your audience begins to trust your brand as a reliable source of information. Authority enhances credibility, making customers more likely to choose your products or services over competitors.

3. Engaging and Retaining Customers

Engaging content keeps your audience interested and encourages them to interact with your brand. Whether through blog posts, social media updates, videos, or newsletters, consistent engagement fosters a sense of community and loyalty. This ongoing relationship helps in retaining customers and turning them into repeat buyers and brand advocates.

4. Supporting SEO Efforts

Search engines reward websites that regularly publish relevant, high-quality content. By optimizing your content for relevant keywords and ensuring it meets user intent, you can improve your rankings on search engine results pages. Higher rankings lead to increased organic traffic, which is a sustainable and cost-effective way to attract potential customers.

5. Nurturing Leads and Driving Conversions

Content marketing plays a crucial role in nurturing leads through the sales funnel. By providing valuable information that addresses your audience's pain points and needs, you can guide them through the buyer's journey. Well-crafted content with clear calls-to-action (CTAs) can lead to higher conversion rates, as it encourages potential customers to take the next step, whether it's subscribing to a newsletter, downloading a resource, or making a purchase.

6. Cost-Effectiveness

Compared to traditional marketing methods, content marketing can be more cost-effective. While there is an upfront investment in creating quality content, the long-term benefits often outweigh the costs. Content can be repurposed and shared across multiple platforms, maximizing its reach and impact without a proportional increase in expenditure.

7. Enhancing Customer Experience

Quality content enhances the overall customer experience by providing valuable information and solutions. Content that educates, entertains, or inspires your audience helps build a positive relationship with your brand. When customers feel informed and supported, they are more likely to have a favorable view of your business and remain loyal.

8. Building Trust and Loyalty

Trust is a critical factor in the buying process. By consistently delivering valuable content, you build trust with your audience. Transparent and honest content, such as case studies, testimonials, and behind-the-scenes looks, helps in creating an authentic brand image. Trust leads to loyalty, and loyal customers are more likely to become repeat buyers and brand advocates.

9. Generating Leads and Supporting Sales

Content marketing is a powerful tool for lead generation. By offering valuable resources, such as e-books, webinars, and whitepapers, in exchange for contact information, you can grow your email list and generate leads. These leads can then be nurtured with targeted content that guides them through the sales funnel, ultimately driving sales and revenue.

10. Staying Competitive

In today's digital landscape, businesses that effectively utilize content marketing have a competitive edge. Content allows you to differentiate your brand, showcase your unique value proposition, and connect with your audience on a deeper level. By staying ahead of content marketing trends and continuously improving your strategy, you can maintain a competitive advantage in your industry.

11. Supporting Other Marketing Strategies

Content marketing complements and enhances other marketing strategies, such as social media marketing, email marketing, and paid advertising. High-quality content provides the foundation for successful campaigns across these channels. For example, engaging blog posts can be shared on social media to drive traffic, while informative articles can be included in email newsletters to nurture leads.

THE ROLE OF CONTENT IN THE BUYER'S JOURNEY

The buyer's journey is a framework that illustrates the stages a potential customer goes through before making a purchase decision. Content marketing plays a critical role in guiding prospects through this journey by providing relevant information and solutions at each stage. The journey typically consists of three main stages: Awareness, Consideration, and Decision. Let's explore how content fits into each of these stages.

1. Awareness Stage - the objective is to attract and educate

In the awareness stage, potential customers realize they have a problem or need but may not yet understand it fully or know the potential solutions. The goal at this stage is to attract attention and educate the audience about their problems and possible solutions.

Types of Content:
- **Blog Posts:** Informative articles that address common questions or pain points.
- **Infographics:** Visual content that simplifies complex information and captures attention.
- **E-books and Guides:** In-depth resources that provide a comprehensive overview of a topic.
- **Videos:** Short, engaging videos that introduce the problem and potential solutions.
- **Social Media Posts:** Content that sparks curiosity and drives traffic to your website.

Example: A company that sells eco-friendly cleaning products might create blog posts about the harmful effects of conventional cleaning products on health and the environment. They could also produce an infographic showing the benefits of using green cleaning alternatives.

2. Consideration Stage - the objective is to inform and persuade

In the consideration stage, potential customers are actively seeking solutions to their problem. They are comparing different options and considering which one might be the best fit. The goal at this stage is to inform and persuade by highlighting the benefits and features of your product or service.

Types of Content:
- **Case Studies:** Real-life examples of how your product or service has helped other customers.
- **Webinars:** Interactive sessions that provide detailed information and allow for live Q&A.
- **Whitepapers:** In-depth reports that explore specific topics and demonstrate expertise.
- **Comparison Guides:** Documents that compare your offerings with competitors, highlighting your unique advantages.
- **Product Demonstration Videos:** Videos that showcase how your product works and its benefits.

Example: The eco-friendly cleaning products company might create a case study showing how a small business switched to their products and saw improvements in employee health and environmental impact. They could also host a webinar discussing the science behind their products' effectiveness.

3. Decision Stage - the objective is to convert and encourage action

In the decision stage, potential customers are ready to make a purchase decision. They need reassurance that they are making the right choice. The goal at this stage is to convert prospects into customers by providing content that builds trust and encourages action.

Types of Content:
- **Testimonials and Reviews:** Customer feedback that builds trust and credibility.
- **Detailed Product Pages:** Comprehensive pages that provide all necessary information, including specifications, pricing, and FAQs.
- **Free Trials or Demos:** Opportunities for potential customers to experience the product firsthand.
- **Discounts and Offers:** Special promotions that incentivize immediate action.
- **FAQ Pages:** Answers to common questions that address any remaining doubts.

Example: The eco-friendly cleaning products company could feature testimonials from satisfied customers on their website and offer a limited-time discount for first-time buyers. They might also provide a free sample pack so prospects can try the products before committing.

CHAPTER 2

Developing a Content Strategy

SETTING CLEAR GOALS & OBJECTIVES

Setting clear goals and objectives is the foundation of a successful content strategy. Without well-defined goals, it's challenging to measure the effectiveness of your content efforts and make informed adjustments.

1. Understanding the Importance of Goals and Objectives
Goals and objectives provide direction and focus for your content marketing efforts. They help you determine what you want to achieve and how you plan to get there. Clear goals ensure that all team members are aligned and working towards the same outcomes, making your strategy more cohesive and effective.

2. Differentiating Between Goals and Objectives
Goals: Broad, long-term outcomes you want to achieve. They are the overarching results that guide your content marketing efforts.

Objectives: Specific, measurable actions you take to achieve your goals. They are detailed and time-bound, providing a clear path to reaching your goals.

Example:
- Goal: Increase brand awareness.
- Objective: Publish 12 high-quality blog posts per month to increase website traffic by 25% within six months.

3. Aligning Goals with Business Objectives

Ensure that your content marketing goals are aligned with your overall business objectives. This alignment ensures that your content efforts contribute to the broader success of your organization. Start by understanding your company's mission, vision, and business goals, then identify how content marketing can support these areas.

Example:

- Business Objective: Increase market share in the eco-friendly products sector.

- Content Marketing Goal: Position the brand as a thought leader in sustainability.

- Objective: Publish 20 in-depth articles on sustainability practices and trends over the next year.

4. SMART Goals Framework

Use the SMART criteria to set clear and achievable goals:
Specific: Define your goals clearly and precisely.

Measurable: Ensure you can track and measure your progress.

Achievable: Set realistic goals that are attainable.

Relevant: Align your goals with broader business objectives.

Time-bound: Set deadlines to achieve your goals.

Example:

- Goal: Increase email newsletter subscriptions.
- SMART Goal: Grow the email subscriber list by 15% in the next three months by offering exclusive content and promotions.

5. Identifying Key Performance Indicators (KPIs)

Key Performance Indicators (KPIs) are metrics that help you measure the success of your content marketing efforts. Select KPIs that align with your goals and provide actionable insights.

Common KPIs:
- Website traffic
- Social media engagement
- Email open and click-through rates
- Conversion rates
- Lead generation
- Customer retention

Example:
- Goal: Improve lead generation.
- KPI: Number of new leads generated through gated content downloads.

6. Establishing Benchmarks and Baselines

Before implementing your content strategy, establish benchmarks and baselines to understand your starting point. This data helps you measure progress and evaluate the effectiveness of your efforts.

Steps to Establish Benchmarks:
- Analyze current performance metrics.
- Identify industry standards and competitor performance.
- Set realistic benchmarks based on your analysis.

Example:
- Benchmark: Current website traffic is 10,000 visitors per month.
- Goal: Increase traffic by 20% within six months.
- Objective: Implement a content promotion strategy to drive an additional 2,000 visitors per month.

7. Reviewing and Adjusting Goals

Regularly review your goals and objectives to ensure they remain relevant and achievable. The digital marketing landscape is dynamic, and your content strategy should be flexible enough to adapt to changes. Use performance data to refine your goals and make necessary adjustments.

Review Process:
- Schedule regular performance reviews (e.g., monthly, quarterly).

- Analyze KPI data and compare it against your benchmarks.

- Identify areas for improvement and adjust goals accordingly.

Example:
- Initial Goal: Increase social media followers by 10% in three months.

- Adjustment: After reviewing performance, adjust the goal to focus on engagement rather than just follower growth.

IDENTIFYING AND UNDERSTANDING YOUR TARGET AUDIENCE

Understanding your target audience is a critical step in developing a successful content strategy. Your audience's needs, preferences, and behaviors should guide the creation and distribution of your content.

1. Importance of Knowing Your Audience

Knowing your audience allows you to create content that is relevant, engaging, and valuable. When you understand who your audience is, you can tailor your messaging, tone, and content formats to meet their specific needs and preferences. This targeted approach increases the likelihood of your content being well-received and achieving your marketing goals.

2. Conducting Audience Research

Start by gathering data about your current and potential audience. Use a combination of qualitative and quantitative research methods to build a comprehensive understanding.

Methods of Audience Research:
- **Surveys and Questionnaires:** Collect direct feedback from your audience about their preferences, challenges, and interests.
- **Interviews:** Conduct in-depth interviews with a representative sample of your audience to gain deeper insights.
- **Analytics Tools:** Use tools like Google Analytics, social media analytics, and email marketing metrics to gather data on audience behavior and demographics.
- **Market Research Reports:** Review industry reports and studies to understand broader market trends and consumer behavior.
- **Competitor Analysis:** Analyze your competitors' audiences to identify potential gaps and opportunities in the market.

3. Creating Buyer Personas

Buyer personas are semi-fictional representations of your ideal customers based on real data and insights. They help you humanize your audience and understand their motivations, pain points, and behaviors.

Steps to Create Buyer Personas:
- **Demographic Information:** Age, gender, location, education level, job title, and income.
- **Psychographic Information:** Interests, values, attitudes, and lifestyle.
- **Behavioral Information:** Buying habits, brand loyalty, and decision-making processes.
- **Pain Points:** Common challenges or problems your audience faces.
- **Goals and Aspirations:** What your audience hopes to achieve and their long-term objectives.

Simple Buyer Persona Example

- **Name:** Eco-conscious Emma
- **Age:** 28
- **Location:** Seattle, WA
- **Occupation:** Marketing Manager
- **Interests:** Sustainability, outdoor activities, organic food
- **Pain Points:** Difficulty finding affordable eco-friendly products
- **Goals:** Reduce environmental footprint, support sustainable brands

Complex Buyer Persona Example

Name: Tech-Savvy Tom

Age: 34

Location: San Francisco, CA

Occupation: Senior Software Engineer at a Mid-sized Tech Company

Income: $120,000 per year

Education: Bachelor's degree in Computer Science

Family Status: Married, no children

Interests and Hobbies:
- Passionate about the latest technology and gadgets
- Enjoys coding and participating in hackathons
- Loves outdoor activities like hiking and cycling
- Active in online gaming communities
- Regularly attends tech conferences and meetups

Lifestyle:

- Lives in an urban apartment equipped with smart home devices
- Favors convenience and efficiency in daily routines
- Health-conscious and prefers organic food
- Environmentally aware and supports sustainable brands

Behavioral Traits:

- Early adopter of new technologies and products
- Frequently shops online, especially for tech gadgets and accessories
- Relies heavily on online reviews and peer recommendations before making a purchase
- Engages with brands on social media, particularly LinkedIn and Twitter
- Subscribes to tech blogs, podcasts, and YouTube channels for industry updates

Values and Motivations:

- Values innovation, efficiency, and quality
- Motivated by the desire to stay ahead of tech trends and continuously improve his skills
- Appreciates brands that demonstrate transparency and ethical practices
- Seeks products that enhance productivity and integrate seamlessly into his tech-driven lifestyle

Pain Points:

- Frustrated by products that are not user-friendly or lack integration with existing systems
- Concerned about data privacy and security with new tech products
- Finds it challenging to stay updated with rapidly changing technology trends
- Dislikes poor customer service and long response times from tech support

Goals and Aspirations:
- Wants to advance his career by staying updated with the latest technologies and earning industry certifications
- Aspires to develop a personal tech blog or YouTube channel to share his expertise
- Aims to automate more aspects of his home and life for greater convenience
- Hopes to start a tech consultancy business in the future

Preferred Content Formats:
- In-depth blog posts and technical articles
- Video tutorials and webinars
- Interactive product demos and live Q&A sessions
- Detailed case studies and whitepapers
- Engaging infographics and visual content

Preferred Communication Channels:
- Email newsletters with personalized content
- Professional networks like LinkedIn
- Tech forums and online communities (e.g., Reddit, Stack Overflow)
- Social media platforms (primarily Twitter for tech news and updates)
- Video platforms like YouTube for tutorials and product reviews

Marketing Messages:
- Emphasize the innovative features and technical specifications of products
- Highlight case studies and success stories of how your products have helped similar professionals
- Provide detailed comparisons with competitor products, focusing on unique benefits and superior performance
- Address data privacy and security measures to alleviate concerns
- Offer exclusive access to beta testing and early product releases to appeal to his early adopter nature

Customer Journey:
- Awareness: Discovers your brand through a tech blog or YouTube review
- Consideration: Researches your products by reading detailed reviews and watching comparison videos
- Decision: Signs up for a webinar or downloads a whitepaper to gain deeper insights before making a purchase
- Retention: Engages with your brand through personalized email updates and participates in user forums or online communities
- Advocacy: Shares positive experiences on social media and recommends your products to peers in tech communities

4. Segmenting Your Audience

Not all members of your audience will have the same needs or interests. Segment your audience into smaller, more specific groups to create targeted content that resonates with each segment.

Segmentation Criteria:
- **Demographic Segmentation:** Age, gender, income, education, etc.
- **Geographic Segmentation:** Location, climate, urban vs. rural, etc.
- **Psychographic Segmentation:** Lifestyle, values, personality, etc.
- **Behavioral Segmentation:** Purchasing behavior, user status, loyalty, etc.

Example Segments:
- Young professionals interested in sustainability
- Parents looking for eco-friendly products for their children
- Business owners seeking sustainable business solutions

5. Understanding Audience Needs and Preferences

Dive deeper into what your audience cares about and what kind of content they prefer. Use your research findings to identify key topics, formats, and channels that will be most effective.

Questions to Consider:
- What problems or challenges is your audience facing?
- What questions do they frequently ask?
- What type of content do they engage with the most (blogs, videos, infographics, etc.)?
- Which social media platforms do they use?
- What time of day are they most active online?

6. Monitoring and Updating Audience Insights

Audience preferences and behaviors can change over time. Continuously monitor your audience and update your personas and segments to reflect these changes.

Monitoring Techniques:
- **Regular Surveys:** Periodically ask your audience for feedback.
- **Social Listening:** Monitor social media conversations to understand emerging trends and sentiments.
- **Website Analytics:** Track how users interact with your content and adjust accordingly.
- **Content Performance:** Analyze which content pieces perform best and why.

CONDUCTING A CONTENT AUDIT

A content audit is a comprehensive review of all the content your organization has produced and published. It helps you assess the current state of your content, identify gaps, and develop a strategy for future content creation. Conducting a content audit is crucial for understanding what is working, what needs improvement, and where there are opportunities for new content.

Here's a step-by-step guide to conducting an effective content audit.

1. Define Your Goals and Scope

Before starting the content audit, it's essential to define what you hope to achieve. This will help you stay focused and ensure that your audit is aligned with your overall content strategy.

Common Goals for a Content Audit:
- Improve SEO performance
- Enhance user engagement
- Identify content gaps and opportunities
- Streamline content production processes
- Align content with brand messaging and goals

Scope of the Audit:
- Decide which types of content to include (e.g., blog posts, videos, infographics, social media posts).
- Determine the timeframe for the audit (e.g., the past year, all content to date).

2. Inventory Your Content

Collect all the content you want to audit. This can be done manually or using tools that help gather and organize your content.

Steps to Inventory Your Content:
- List all URLs of your web pages, blog posts, and other online content.
- Include metadata such as publication date, author, content type, and categories.
- Use tools like Google Analytics, Screaming Frog, or content management system (CMS) exports to simplify this process.

3. Categorize and Tag Your Content

Organize your content into relevant categories and tag it based on specific attributes. This helps in analyzing the content more effectively.

Common Categories and Tags:
- Content type (blog post, video, infographic, etc.)
- Topic or theme
- Buyer's journey stage (awareness, consideration, decision)
- Performance metrics (views, shares, conversions)
- Target audience or persona

4. Analyze Content Performance

Evaluate the performance of each piece of content using key metrics. This analysis will help you understand what content resonates with your audience and meets your goals.

Key Performance Metrics:
- Traffic: Number of page views, unique visitors
- Engagement: Time on page, bounce rate, comments, social shares
- SEO: Organic search traffic, keyword rankings, backlinks
- Conversions: Leads generated, conversion rate, call-to-action (CTA) effectiveness.

Tools for Performance Analysis:
- Google Analytics for website performance
- SEMrush or Ahrefs for SEO metrics
- Social media analytics for engagement on social platforms
- Email marketing software for email content performance

5. Assess Content Quality and Relevance

Beyond quantitative metrics, it's important to assess the qualitative aspects of your content. This involves evaluating the quality, relevance, and alignment with your brand and audience needs.

Qualitative Assessment Criteria:
- Content Quality: Is the content well-written, accurate, and free of errors?
- Relevance: Is the content still relevant to your audience? Does it address their current needs and interests?
- Brand Alignment: Does the content reflect your brand's voice, tone, and messaging?
- User Experience: Is the content easy to read and navigate? Does it include multimedia elements that enhance engagement?

6. Identify Gaps and Opportunities

Based on your analysis, identify areas where your content is lacking and opportunities for new content. Look for gaps in topics, formats, and stages of the buyer's journey.

Common Gaps to Look For:
- Topics that are underrepresented or missing
- Content types that are lacking (e.g., videos, infographics)
- Stages of the buyer's journey with insufficient content
- Audience segments that are not adequately addressed

7. Develop Actionable Insights and Recommendations

Summarize your findings and develop actionable insights to improve your content strategy. Make specific recommendations for updating, repurposing, or creating new content.

Recommendations May Include:
- Content Updates: Refresh outdated content with new information and visuals.
- Content Repurposing: Transform high-performing content into different formats (e.g., turning a blog post into a video).
- New Content Creation: Plan new content to fill identified gaps and meet audience needs.
- SEO Enhancements: Optimize content for better search performance by adding keywords, updating meta descriptions, and improving internal linking.

8. Create a Content Audit Report

Compile your findings and recommendations into a comprehensive report. This report should be clear, concise, and actionable, serving as a guide for your content strategy moving forward.

Components of a Content Audit Report:
- Executive Summary: Brief overview of the audit goals, scope, and key findings.
- Detailed Analysis: Breakdown of content performance, quality, and relevance.
- Identified Gaps: Summary of content gaps and opportunities.
- Actionable Recommendations: Specific steps to improve and enhance your content strategy.
- Next Steps: Outline of the immediate actions and longer-term plans based on the audit insights.

CREATING A CONTENT CALENDAR

A content calendar is a crucial tool for planning, organizing, and managing your content marketing efforts. It ensures that you consistently publish high-quality content, stay on track with your strategy, and align your content with your business goals and audience needs. This section will guide you through the process of creating an effective content calendar.

1. Importance of a Content Calendar

A content calendar provides numerous benefits:

- Organization: Helps you keep track of all content initiatives and deadlines.
- Consistency: Ensures regular publishing, which is critical for maintaining audience engagement and improving SEO.
- Planning: Allows for strategic planning of content themes, formats, and channels.
- Alignment: Ensures content aligns with marketing campaigns, product launches, and key business events.
- Accountability: Assigns responsibilities and deadlines, ensuring team members know their roles.

2. Define Your Goals and Objectives

Before creating your content calendar, define your content marketing goals and objectives. These should align with your overall business goals and audience needs.

Example Goals:

- Increase website traffic by 20% in six months.
- Generate 100 new leads per month.
- Boost social media engagement by 15% in three months.

3. Choose Your Content Calendar Format

Select a format that suits your team's workflow. Options include:

- Spreadsheet: Simple and customizable (e.g., Google Sheets, Excel).
- Calendar Apps: Visual and easy to use (e.g., Google Calendar, Outlook).
- Project Management Tools: Integrated features for team collaboration (e.g., Trello, Asana, Monday.com).
- Business Suite (schedule it directly on Facebook & Instagram)
- Third party tools, which also help schedule to all channels (e.g. Sprout Social)

4. Plan Your Content Themes and Topics

Identify overarching themes and specific topics that align with your goals and audience interests. Consider seasonal trends, industry events, and product launches.

Example Themes:
- Sustainability (January)
- Tech Innovations (February)
- Customer Success Stories (March)

5. Determine Content Types and Formats

Diversify your content to cater to different audience preferences and platforms. Plan a mix of blog posts, videos, infographics, podcasts, social media updates, and more.

Example Formats:
- Blog post every Monday
- Video tutorial every Wednesday
- Infographic every Friday
- Social media posts daily

6. Assign Content Creation Responsibilities

If you have a team who carries out the content efforts, clearly define who is responsible for each piece of content so the process runs smoothly. This ensures accountability and helps manage workloads.

Roles to Assign:
- Content Creator: Researches and writes content.
- Editor: Reviews and edits content for quality and accuracy.
- Designer: Creates visuals and multimedia elements.
- Social Media Manager: Schedules and promotes content on social platforms.
- SEO Specialist: Optimizes content for search engines.

7. Set Deadlines and Publishing Dates

Establish deadlines for each stage of the content creation process, from initial drafts to final publication. Include buffer time for revisions and approvals.

Example Timeline:
- Topic brainstorming: First week of the month
- Draft submission: By the 10th of each month
- Editing and revisions: 11th-15th of the month
- Final approval: 16th of the month
- Publishing date: 17th of the month

8. Incorporate SEO and Keywords

Integrate keyword research into your content planning to improve SEO. Ensure that each piece of content targets relevant keywords and includes optimized meta descriptions, titles, and headers.

Example Keyword Plan:
- January blog post: "Sustainable business practices" (keyword: sustainable business)
- February video: "Latest tech innovations in 2024" (keyword: tech innovations 2024)

9. Plan for Content Promotion

Outline your content promotion strategy within your calendar. This includes social media promotion, email marketing, paid ads, and influencer collaborations.

Example Promotion Plan:
- Blog post promotion on LinkedIn and Twitter: 17th-19th of the month
- Email newsletter featuring new content: 20th of the month
- Paid ad campaign for video tutorial: 21st-30th of the month

10. Review and Adjust Regularly

Regularly review your content calendar to assess performance and make adjustments. Use analytics to track the success of your content and refine your strategy based on data.

Review Process:
- Weekly check-ins to ensure deadlines are met.
- Monthly reviews to assess performance metrics.
- Quarterly strategy meetings to adjust content themes and goals.

CHAPTER 3

Types of Content and Their Uses

BLOG POSTS

Blog posts are one of the most versatile and effective types of content in a digital marketing strategy. They serve multiple purposes, from attracting organic traffic and engaging your audience to establishing your brand as an authority in your industry.

1. Benefits of Blog Posts

a. Driving Organic Traffic:
  - Well-optimized blog posts can rank high on search engine results pages (SERPs), attracting organic traffic to your website.
  - By targeting relevant keywords, you can reach potential customers who are searching for information related to your products or services.

b. Building Authority and Credibility:
  - Regularly publishing high-quality blog posts positions your brand as a thought leader in your industry.
  - Providing valuable insights and solutions to your audience's problems builds trust and establishes your credibility.

c. Engaging Your Audience:
  - Blog posts allow you to connect with your audience on a deeper level by addressing their needs, interests, and pain points.
  - Encouraging comments and interactions on your blog posts fosters a sense of community and engagement.

d. Supporting Other Marketing Efforts:

- Blog content can be repurposed for social media posts, email newsletters, and other marketing channels.
- Internal linking within blog posts improves SEO and keeps visitors on your website longer, increasing the chances of conversion.

2. Best Practices for Creating Blog Posts

a. Understanding Your Audience:

- Conduct thorough research to understand your audience's needs, preferences, and pain points.
- Create buyer personas to guide your content creation and ensure relevance.

b. Crafting Compelling Headlines:

- Headlines are the first thing readers see, so make them attention-grabbing and relevant.
- Use power words, numbers, and clear benefits to entice readers to click.

c. Writing High-Quality Content:

- Focus on providing value through well-researched, informative, and actionable content.
- Maintain a clear and engaging writing style that resonates with your audience.

d. Incorporating Visuals:

- Use images, infographics, and videos to break up text and enhance the visual appeal of your blog posts.
- Visuals help illustrate points, improve understanding, and keep readers engaged.

e. Structuring Your Posts:
   - Use subheadings, bullet points, and short paragraphs to make your content easy to read and scan.
   - Include a clear introduction, body, and conclusion to provide structure and flow.

3. Optimizing Blog Posts for SEO

a. Keyword Research:
   - Identify relevant keywords that your audience is searching for using tools like Google Keyword Planner, SEMrush, or Ahrefs.
   - Focus on long-tail keywords that are specific and less competitive.

b. On-Page SEO:
   - Include your target keyword in the title, headers, and throughout the content naturally.
   - Optimize meta descriptions, alt text for images, and URL slugs for better search engine visibility.

c. Internal and External Linking:
   - Link to other relevant blog posts and pages on your website to improve SEO and keep visitors engaged.
   - Include external links to reputable sources to add credibility and provide additional value to your readers.

d. Mobile Optimization:
   - Ensure your blog posts are mobile-friendly, as a significant portion of users access content on mobile devices.
   - Use responsive design and optimize loading times for a better user experience.

4. Promoting Your Blog Posts

a. Social Media:
   - Share your blog posts on various social media platforms to reach a broader audience.
   - Use engaging captions, hashtags, and visuals to attract attention and encourage sharing.

b. Email Marketing:
   - Include links to your latest blog posts in your email newsletters to drive traffic and keep your subscribers engaged.
   - Use compelling subject lines and teasers to entice recipients to read your blog posts.

c. Content Syndication:
   - Syndicate your blog posts on platforms like Medium or LinkedIn to increase visibility and reach new audiences.
   - Ensure you follow best practices for content syndication to avoid duplicate content issues.

d. Influencer Outreach:
   - Collaborate with industry influencers to promote your blog posts and reach their followers.
   - Offer value to influencers by providing high-quality content that resonates with their audience.

5. Measuring the Success of Your Blog Posts

a. Key Performance Indicators (KPIs):
   - Track metrics such as page views, time on page, bounce rate, and social shares to gauge the performance of your blog posts.
   - Monitor conversion rates and lead generation to measure the impact on your business goals.

b. Analytics Tools:

- Use Google Analytics to gain insights into your blog's performance and understand user behavior.
- Leverage tools like SEMrush or Ahrefs to track keyword rankings and SEO performance.

c. Continuous Improvement:

- Regularly review your blog's performance and identify areas for improvement.
- Update old blog posts with new information, optimize for new keywords, and refresh visuals to keep content relevant.

INFOGRAPHICS

Infographics are a highly effective content type that combines visuals and text to convey information in a clear, engaging, and easily digestible format. They are particularly useful for presenting complex data, illustrating processes, and summarizing information.

1. Benefits of Infographics

a. Simplifying Complex Information:

- Infographics break down complex data and concepts into visual elements that are easier to understand.
- They use visuals like charts, graphs, and icons to represent information succinctly.

b. Enhancing Engagement:

- The visual appeal of infographics captures attention and encourages sharing.
- They can make dry or technical subjects more interesting and engaging for the audience.

c. Increasing Shareability:
- Infographics are highly shareable on social media platforms, increasing your content's reach.
- They are often cited and linked to by other websites, which can enhance your SEO.

d. Establishing Authority:
- Creating well-researched and high-quality infographics positions your brand as an expert in your industry.
- They demonstrate your ability to distill and present valuable information effectively.

2. Best Practices for Creating Infographics

a. Identify Your Purpose and Audience:
- Clearly define the purpose of the infographic and the specific audience it is intended for.
- Tailor the content and design to meet the needs and preferences of your target audience.

b. Choose a Relevant Topic:
- Select a topic that is relevant to your audience and aligns with your content strategy.
- Consider trending topics, frequently asked questions, and evergreen content that will remain useful over time.

c. Conduct Thorough Research:
- Gather accurate and reliable data from reputable sources to support the information presented in the infographic.
- Ensure the data is up-to-date and properly cited to maintain credibility.

d. Create a Compelling Design:

- Use a clean and visually appealing design that highlights key information and guides the viewer's eye.
- Incorporate a consistent color scheme, typography, and branding elements that align with your brand identity.

e. Focus on Clarity and Simplicity:

- Avoid overcrowding the infographic with too much information or complex visuals.
- Use clear headings, subheadings, and concise text to make the content easy to follow.

f. Utilize Visual Elements Effectively:

- Employ charts, graphs, icons, and illustrations to represent data and concepts visually.
- Use visual hierarchy to prioritize important information and guide the viewer's attention.

3. Tools for Creating Infographics

Several tools can help you create professional and visually appealing infographics, even if you don't have extensive design experience:

a. Canva:

- A user-friendly design tool with a wide range of templates and customization options.
- Ideal for creating infographics quickly and easily.

b. Piktochart:

- Offers a variety of templates and design elements specifically for infographics.
- Allows for easy integration of charts and data visualization.

c. Adobe Illustrator:
- A powerful design tool for creating highly customized and detailed infographics.
- Suitable for those with advanced design skills.

d. Venngage:
- Provides templates, icons, and data visualization tools tailored for infographics.
- Great for creating professional-looking infographics with ease.

4. Promoting Your Infographics

a. Social Media:
- Share your infographics on platforms like Instagram, Pinterest, LinkedIn, and Facebook.
- Use relevant hashtags, engaging captions, and call-to-actions to increase visibility and engagement.

b. Blog Posts:
- Embed infographics within related blog posts to enhance the content and provide visual interest.
- Create blog posts specifically about the infographic topic, offering additional context and analysis.

c. Email Marketing:
- Include infographics in your email newsletters to make your emails more engaging and informative.
- Use eye-catching designs to draw attention and encourage clicks.

d. Content Syndication:

- Share your infographics on content syndication platforms like SlideShare or Medium.
- Reach a broader audience and drive traffic back to your website.

e. Influencer Outreach:

- Collaborate with industry influencers to share your infographics with their audience.
- Offer value by providing high-quality, shareable content that resonates with their followers.

5. Measuring the Success of Your Infographics

a. Key Performance Indicators (KPIs):

- Track metrics such as shares, likes, comments, and mentions on social media.
- Monitor website traffic, time on page, and bounce rates for pages featuring infographics.

b. Analytics Tools:

- Use Google Analytics to measure the impact of infographics on website traffic and user engagement.
- Leverage social media analytics to assess the reach and interaction of your infographics.

c. Continuous Improvement:

- Analyze performance data to identify what works and what doesn't.
- Gather feedback from your audience and use it to improve future infographics.

E-BOOKS AND WHITEPAPERS

E-books and whitepapers are in-depth content formats that provide detailed information, analysis, and insights on specific topics. They are valuable assets in a content marketing strategy, helping to establish authority, generate leads, and nurture prospects through the buyer's journey.

1. Benefits of E-books and Whitepapers

a. Establishing Authority and Expertise:
  - E-books and whitepapers allow you to showcase your knowledge and expertise on a particular subject.
  - By providing comprehensive and well-researched information, you position your brand as a thought leader in your industry.

b. Generating Leads:
  - Offering e-books and whitepapers as gated content (requiring users to provide contact information) helps generate qualified leads.
  - These formats attract users who are genuinely interested in the topic, increasing the likelihood of conversion.

c. Providing Value and Education:
  - E-books and whitepapers offer substantial value by educating your audience on complex topics.
  - They help build trust and credibility with your audience, fostering long-term relationships.

d. Supporting the Buyer's Journey:
 - These formats are particularly effective during the consideration and decision stages of the buyer's journey.
 - They provide in-depth information that helps prospects make informed decisions about your products or services.

2. Best Practices for Creating E-books and Whitepapers

a. Choose Relevant and Valuable Topics:
 - Select topics that are relevant to your audience's needs, challenges, and interests.
 - Conduct research to identify trending topics, frequently asked questions, and industry pain points.

b. Conduct Thorough Research:
 - Gather accurate and credible information from reputable sources to support your content.
 - Ensure your e-book or whitepaper is well-researched, comprehensive, and provides actionable insights.

c. Create a Detailed Outline:
 - Develop a clear and logical structure for your content, including an introduction, main body, and conclusion.
 - Break down the content into sections and subsections to make it easier to follow.

d. Write in an Engaging and Professional Tone:
 - Use a tone that reflects your brand's voice while maintaining a professional and authoritative style.
 - Ensure the content is clear, concise, and free of jargon that might confuse readers.

e. Design for Readability and Visual Appeal:

- Use a clean and professional design with consistent branding elements such as colors, fonts, and logos.
- Incorporate visuals like charts, graphs, images, and infographics to enhance understanding and break up text.

f. Include a Strong Call-to-Action (CTA):

- Guide readers to the next step, whether it's downloading another resource, signing up for a newsletter, or contacting your sales team.
- Make your CTA clear, compelling, and easy to follow.

3. Promoting E-books and Whitepapers

a. Landing Pages:

- Create dedicated landing pages for each e-book or whitepaper with persuasive copy and a clear CTA.
- Use forms to capture contact information in exchange for the download.

b. Email Marketing:

- Promote your e-books and whitepapers through email campaigns targeting your existing subscribers.
- Use engaging subject lines and previews to entice recipients to download the content.

c. Social Media:

- Share your e-books and whitepapers on social media platforms with eye-catching visuals and compelling captions.
- Use relevant hashtags and encourage sharing to increase visibility.

d. Content Syndication:
- Syndicate your e-books and whitepapers on platforms like LinkedIn, SlideShare, and Medium to reach a broader audience.
- Ensure you include links back to your website or landing pages.

e. Paid Advertising:
- Use pay-per-click (PPC) campaigns on Google Ads and social media platforms to promote your e-books and whitepapers.
- Target specific demographics and interests to reach your ideal audience.

f. Influencer and Partner Collaborations:
- Partner with industry influencers or complementary businesses to co-create and promote your e-books and whitepapers.
- Leverage their audience to increase reach and credibility.

4. Measuring the Success of E-books and Whitepapers

a. Key Performance Indicators (KPIs):
- Track the number of downloads and leads generated.
- Monitor engagement metrics such as time spent on the landing page and click-through rates.

b. Analytics Tools:
- Use tools like Google Analytics to track traffic sources, user behavior, and conversion rates.
- Leverage marketing automation platforms to monitor the performance of email campaigns and landing pages.

c. Continuous Improvement:
- Gather feedback from your audience to understand what they found valuable and where improvements can be made.
- Regularly update your e-books and whitepapers with new information and insights to keep them relevant.

CASE STUDIES AND TESTIMONIALS

Case studies and testimonials are powerful content formats that highlight real-life success stories and positive experiences of your customers. They serve as social proof, demonstrating the value and effectiveness of your products or services.

1. Benefits of Case Studies and Testimonials

a. Building Trust and Credibility:
- Showcasing real customer experiences helps build trust with potential customers.
- Case studies and testimonials provide third-party validation, making your claims more credible.

b. Demonstrating Results:
- They offer concrete examples of how your product or service has solved problems and delivered results.
- Detailed success stories help potential customers envision similar outcomes for themselves.

c. Addressing Objections:
- By sharing stories from customers who had similar concerns or objections, you can address potential doubts.
- Testimonials from satisfied customers can reassure prospects and alleviate fears.

d. Enhancing SEO and Lead Generation:
   - Well-crafted case studies and testimonials can improve your website's SEO, attracting more organic traffic.
   - They can serve as valuable lead magnets when offered as downloadable content.

2. Best Practices for Creating Case Studies

a. Choose the Right Customers:
   - Select customers who have had significant success with your product or service.
   - Ensure they represent your target audience and have relatable challenges and outcomes.

b. Develop a Structured Format:
   - Use a consistent format to make your case studies easy to read and compare.
   - Include sections such as Background, Challenge, Solution, and Results.

c. Focus on Storytelling:
   - Craft a compelling narrative that highlights the customer's journey and transformation.
   - Use quotes and anecdotes from the customer to add authenticity and personal touch.

d. Provide Quantifiable Results:
   - Include specific metrics and data to illustrate the impact of your solution.
   - Highlight measurable outcomes such as increased revenue, cost savings, or improved efficiency.

e. Include Visuals:
   - Use images, charts, and graphs to support your story and make the content more engaging.
   - Visuals help break up text and emphasize key points.

3. Best Practices for Creating Testimonials

a. Request Authentic Testimonials:
   - Ask satisfied customers to share their honest feedback about their experience.
   - Encourage them to highlight specific benefits and outcomes they've experienced.

b. Use a Variety of Formats:
   - Collect testimonials in different formats, including written quotes, video testimonials, and social media mentions.
   - Video testimonials can be particularly impactful due to their personal and visual nature.

c. Highlight Key Points:
   - Focus on specific aspects of your product or service that had the most significant impact on the customer.
   - Emphasize unique features, exceptional service, or outstanding results.

d. Ensure Credibility:
   - Include the customer's name, title, company, and photo (with their permission) to add credibility.
   - If possible, provide links to their company website or social media profiles.

4. Promoting Case Studies and Testimonials

a. Website Placement:
- Feature case studies and testimonials prominently on your website, such as on your homepage, product pages, and dedicated testimonial sections.
- Use call-to-actions to encourage visitors to read or watch these success stories.

b. Social Media:
- Share snippets of case studies and testimonials on social media platforms to reach a broader audience.
- Use engaging visuals and quotes to attract attention and encourage sharing.

c. Email Marketing:
- Include case studies and testimonials in your email newsletters to build trust and credibility with your subscribers.
- Highlight different customer success stories in each email to keep content fresh and engaging.

d. Sales Collateral:
- Provide your sales team with case studies and testimonials to use during their interactions with prospects.
- These assets can help address objections and build trust during the sales process.

e. Content Syndication:
- Share your case studies and testimonials on industry forums, blogs, and third-party websites.
- Collaborate with partners and influencers to expand your reach.

5. Measuring the Success of Case Studies and Testimonials

a. Key Performance Indicators (KPIs):
   - Track metrics such as website visits, downloads, social shares, and engagement for case studies.
   - Monitor the impact of testimonials on lead generation, conversion rates, and customer inquiries.

b. Analytics Tools:
   - Use tools like Google Analytics to measure the performance of case study and testimonial pages.
   - Leverage social media analytics to track the reach and engagement of shared content.

c. Continuous Improvement:
   - Gather feedback from your audience to understand what resonates and what can be improved.
   - Regularly update and refresh case studies and testimonials to keep them relevant and impactful.

PODCASTS

Podcasts have become an increasingly popular content format due to their convenience and ability to engage audiences through storytelling and discussion. They offer a unique way to share information, build relationships with listeners, and establish authority in your industry.

1. Benefits of Podcasts

a. Accessibility and Convenience:
- Podcasts can be consumed on the go, whether listeners are commuting, exercising, or doing household chores.
- They provide a hands-free, screen-free way to consume content, fitting seamlessly into busy lifestyles.

b. Building a Personal Connection:
- The audio format allows for a more personal and intimate connection with the audience.
- Listeners often develop a sense of familiarity and trust with the host, strengthening the brand relationship.

c. Establishing Authority and Thought Leadership:
- Hosting or featuring on podcasts allows you to share expertise, insights, and industry knowledge.
- Regularly publishing podcasts helps position you as a thought leader and trusted source of information.

d. Expanding Audience Reach:
- Podcasts can reach new audiences who prefer audio content over written or visual formats.
- They can be distributed across multiple platforms, including Apple Podcasts, Spotify, Google Podcasts, and more.

e. Encouraging Engagement and Community Building:
- Podcasts can spark discussions and interactions through social media, reviews, and listener feedback.
- They foster a sense of community among listeners who share common interests.

2. Best Practices for Creating Podcasts

a. Define Your Purpose and Audience:
- Clearly define the goal of your podcast and identify your target audience.
- Tailor your content to address the interests, needs, and preferences of your listeners.

b. Plan Your Content:
- Develop a content plan and editorial calendar for your podcast episodes.
- Choose topics that are relevant, timely, and valuable to your audience.
- Consider different formats such as interviews, solo episodes, panel discussions, and storytelling.

c. Invest in Quality Equipment:
- Use a good quality microphone, headphones, and recording software to ensure clear and professional audio.
- Consider using pop filters, soundproofing, and audio editing tools to enhance sound quality.

d. Create Engaging and Structured Episodes:
   - Start with a strong introduction that captures attention and outlines what the episode will cover.
   - Maintain a clear structure with a beginning, middle, and end to keep the content organized and engaging.
   - Use storytelling techniques, real-life examples, and expert insights to make the content compelling.

e. Promote Your Podcast:
   - Create eye-catching cover art and write compelling episode descriptions.
   - Promote each episode through your website, social media channels, email newsletters, and other marketing channels.
   - Encourage listeners to subscribe, leave reviews, and share the podcast with their networks.

3. Tools for Creating Podcasts

a. Recording Software:
   - Audacity: A free, open-source audio recording and editing software.
   - GarageBand: A user-friendly recording tool for Mac users.
   - Adobe Audition: A professional audio editing software with advanced features.

b. Hosting Platforms:
   - Libsyn: A popular podcast hosting service with robust analytics and distribution options.
   - Podbean: A hosting platform that offers monetization options and easy distribution.
   - Anchor: A free hosting service with built-in recording and editing tools.

c. Promotion Tools:

- Canva: Create engaging social media graphics and promotional materials.
- Hootsuite: Schedule and manage social media posts promoting your podcast episodes.
- Mailchimp: Send email newsletters featuring new podcast episodes to your subscribers.

4. Promoting Your Podcasts

a. Social Media:

- Share new episodes on social media platforms with engaging visuals and captions.
- Use relevant hashtags and encourage listeners to share their thoughts and feedback.

b. Website and Blog:

- Embed podcast episodes on your website and write accompanying blog posts to provide additional context and value.
- Create a dedicated podcast section on your website to house all episodes and related content.

c. Email Marketing:

- Include links to new episodes in your email newsletters to keep subscribers informed and engaged.
- Offer exclusive content or behind-the-scenes insights to your email subscribers.

d. Podcast Directories:
- Submit your podcast to popular directories such as Apple Podcasts, Spotify, Google Podcasts, Stitcher, and TuneIn.
- Encourage listeners to rate and review your podcast to increase visibility and credibility.

e. Collaborations and Guest Appearances:
- Invite industry experts and influencers as guests on your podcast to provide valuable insights and attract their audience.
- Appear as a guest on other podcasts to expand your reach and introduce your podcast to new listeners.

5. Measuring the Success of Your Podcasts

a. Key Performance Indicators (KPIs):
- Track metrics such as the number of downloads, subscribers, and listener retention rates.
- Monitor engagement metrics such as social media shares, comments, and listener reviews.

b. Analytics Tools:
- Use podcast hosting platforms that offer built-in analytics to track performance.
- Leverage tools like Google Analytics to monitor website traffic driven by your podcast.

c. Continuous Improvement:
- Gather feedback from your audience to understand what they enjoy and where there are opportunities for improvement.
- Regularly review performance data to identify trends and adjust your content strategy accordingly.

NEWSLETTERS

Newsletters are a versatile and powerful tool in content marketing. They help maintain regular communication with your audience, build relationships, and keep your subscribers informed about your brand, products, and industry updates. This section explores the benefits of newsletters, best practices for creating them, and strategies for maximizing their impact.

1. Benefits of Newsletters

a. Building Relationships and Engagement:
- Regular newsletters keep your audience engaged with your brand.
- They help foster a sense of connection and loyalty among subscribers by providing valuable content consistently.

b. Driving Traffic and Conversions:
- Newsletters can drive traffic to your website, blog, and other online assets.
- They can promote products, services, events, and special offers, encouraging conversions and sales.

c. Establishing Authority and Expertise:
- By sharing industry insights, tips, and valuable information, newsletters position your brand as an authority in your field.
- They provide an opportunity to showcase your expertise and build credibility.

d. Personalization and Segmentation:
- Newsletters can be tailored to different segments of your audience, ensuring relevant and personalized content.
- Segmented newsletters result in higher engagement rates and better subscriber satisfaction.

2. Best Practices for Creating Newsletters

a. Define Your Objectives and Audience:
- Clearly outline the goals of your newsletter, such as increasing engagement, driving sales, or building brand awareness.
- Understand your audience's needs, preferences, and pain points to tailor your content accordingly.

b. Craft Compelling Subject Lines:
- Your subject line is the first thing subscribers see, so make it catchy and relevant.
- Use action words, create a sense of urgency, or pique curiosity to encourage opens.

c. Design for Readability and Visual Appeal:
- Use a clean, professional design with a clear structure and hierarchy.
- Include images, headers, and bullet points to break up text and enhance readability.
- Ensure your newsletter is mobile-friendly, as many users will read it on their smartphones.

d. Provide Valuable Content:
- Focus on delivering content that is valuable, informative, and relevant to your audience.
- Mix different types of content, such as articles, tips, industry news, product updates, and personal stories.

e. Include Clear Calls-to-Action (CTAs):
- Each newsletter should have a clear CTA that guides readers on what to do next, whether it's visiting your website, reading a blog post, or making a purchase.
- Make your CTAs prominent and easy to follow.

f. Personalize Your Content:
   - Use personalization techniques to address subscribers by their names and tailor content based on their preferences and behavior.
   - Segment your audience to send targeted newsletters that are more likely to resonate with specific groups.

g. Optimize for Deliverability:
   - Ensure your emails comply with anti-spam laws and best practices to avoid being marked as spam.
   - Use a reputable email service provider (ESP) to manage your newsletters and monitor deliverability rates.

3. Tools for Creating and Managing Newsletters

a. Mailchimp:
A popular email marketing platform with drag-and-drop design tools, automation features, and advanced analytics.

b. MailerLite:
Provides a range of templates, email scheduling, and list management features, ideal for small businesses.

c. HubSpot:
An all-in-one marketing platform offering email marketing, CRM integration, and detailed performance analytics.

d. ConvertKit:
Designed for creators and bloggers, it offers easy-to-use email automation and segmentation features.

e. ActiveCampaign:
Combines email marketing with CRM capabilities, allowing for advanced segmentation and automation.

4. Promoting Your Newsletters

a. Website Sign-Up Forms:
  - Place sign-up forms prominently on your website, such as in the header, footer, or as pop-ups.
  - Offer incentives like exclusive content, discounts, or free resources to encourage sign-ups.

b. Social Media Promotion:
  - Promote your newsletter sign-up on social media platforms with engaging posts and visuals.
  - Use social media ads to reach a broader audience and drive sign-ups.

c. Content Upgrades:
  - Offer content upgrades in your blog posts or articles, where readers can access additional valuable content by subscribing to your newsletter.

d. Collaboration and Partnerships:
  - Partner with other businesses or influencers to cross-promote your newsletters to their audiences.
  - Feature guest content from industry experts to attract their followers.

e. Offline Promotion:
  - Promote your newsletter at events, conferences, and through printed materials.
  - Encourage sign-ups by offering exclusive event-related content or updates.

5. Measuring the Success of Your Newsletters

a. Key Performance Indicators (KPIs):
- Track open rates, click-through rates, conversion rates, and unsubscribe rates to gauge your newsletter's performance.
- Monitor engagement metrics such as social shares and forwards.

b. Analytics Tools:
- Use the analytics features provided by your email service provider to gain insights into subscriber behavior and engagement.
- Leverage tools like Google Analytics to track the traffic driven to your website from your newsletters.

c. Continuous Improvement:
- Regularly review performance data to identify trends and areas for improvement.
- A/B test different subject lines, content formats, and CTAs to optimize your newsletters.
- Gather feedback from your subscribers to understand their preferences and enhance the value of your content.

SHORT AND LONG FORM VIDEO CONTENT

Video content is a dynamic and engaging way to connect with your audience. With the rise of social media platforms like TikTok, Instagram Reels, and YouTube Shorts, short-form videos have become immensely popular. On the other hand, long-form videos, typically found on YouTube, continue to be a powerful tool for in-depth storytelling and education.

1. Benefits of Video Content

a. High Engagement:
   - Videos capture attention quickly and retain it, leading to higher engagement rates compared to text or static images.
   - They are effective for storytelling, demonstrating products, and conveying complex information succinctly.

b. Versatility:
   - Videos can be used across various platforms and formats, from short social media clips to longer educational videos.
   - They cater to different audience preferences and consumption habits.

c. Boosting SEO and Reach:
   - Video content can improve SEO rankings by increasing time spent on your website and lowering bounce rates.
   - Platforms like YouTube are search engines in their own right, providing additional opportunities for visibility and discovery.

2. Short-Form Video Content (Reels, TikToks, Shorts)

a. Characteristics:
   - Duration: Typically 15 to 60 seconds.
   - Format: Vertical, optimized for mobile viewing.
   - Style: Fast-paced, engaging, and often trend-driven.

b. Best Practices for Creating Short-Form Videos:

i. Capture Attention Quickly:
 - The first few seconds are crucial for capturing viewers' attention. Start with a hook that draws them in immediately.

ii. Focus on a Single Message:
 - Keep the content focused and concise. Convey one main idea or message to avoid overwhelming the viewer.

iii. Leverage Trends and Challenges:
 - Participate in trending challenges, use popular sounds, and incorporate current events to increase visibility and engagement.

iv. Use Captions and Text Overlays:
 - Since many users watch videos without sound, use captions and text overlays to ensure your message is understood.

v. Incorporate Call-to-Actions (CTAs):
 - Encourage viewers to take action, such as liking, sharing, following, or visiting your website.

c. Platforms for Short-Form Videos:

i. TikTok:
 - Ideal for reaching a younger, trend-focused audience.
 - Use TikTok's editing tools, filters, and effects to enhance your videos.

ii. Instagram Reels:
 - Great for engaging with your Instagram audience and leveraging existing followers.
 - Integrate Reels into your broader Instagram strategy.

iii. YouTube Shorts:
   - Use Shorts to reach a broader audience on YouTube and drive traffic to your longer videos.
   - Take advantage of YouTube's vast user base and search capabilities.

3. Long-Form Video Content (Classic YouTube Videos)

a. Characteristics:
   - Duration: Typically 5 to 30 minutes, but can be longer for in-depth content.
   - Format: Horizontal, optimized for various devices.
   - Style: More detailed and comprehensive, suitable for tutorials, reviews, and interviews.

b. Best Practices for Creating Long-Form Videos:

i. Plan and Script Your Content:
Outline your video to ensure a clear structure and flow. A script helps maintain focus and coherence.

ii. Invest in Quality Production:
 Good lighting, clear audio, and high-resolution video are essential. Invest in basic equipment or hire a professional if necessary.

iii. Optimize for SEO:
Use relevant keywords in your title, description, and tags. Include a compelling thumbnail and an engaging video description.

iv. Engage Your Audience:
 Start with a strong introduction to hook viewers. Use storytelling techniques and include visuals to keep them engaged.

v. Include CTAs:
 Encourage viewers to subscribe, comment, share, and visit your website. Use YouTube cards and end screens for additional CTAs.

c. Platforms for Long-Form Videos:

i. YouTube:
  - The leading platform for long-form videos, offering vast reach and robust SEO capabilities.
  - Create a content schedule and consistently upload videos to build and maintain an audience.

ii. Vimeo:
  - A professional video platform ideal for high-quality, ad-free viewing experiences.
  - Use Vimeo for showcasing portfolio work, documentaries, and corporate videos.

4. Strategies for Leveraging Video Content

a. Cross-Promotion:
  - Promote your long-form videos on social media by sharing short clips or teasers.
  - Use short-form videos to drive traffic to your YouTube channel or website.

b. Repurposing Content:
  - Break down long-form videos into shorter segments for social media.
  - Expand on short-form video topics in detailed YouTube videos or blog posts.

c. Engaging with Your Audience:
  - Encourage comments and interact with viewers to build a community.
  - Respond to questions and feedback to foster engagement and loyalty.

d. Analyzing Performance:
  - Use analytics tools to track video performance, such as view counts, watch time, and engagement metrics.
  - Adjust your content strategy based on data insights.

CHAPTER 4

Types of Content and Their Uses

UNDERSTANDING STORYTELLING IN MARKETING

Storytelling is a powerful tool in marketing that goes beyond simply conveying information about your products or services. It involves creating a narrative that engages your audience on an emotional level, making your brand memorable and relatable.

1. The Importance of Storytelling in Marketing

a. Emotional Connection:
Stories evoke emotions, which can create a strong bond between your brand and your audience. Emotional connections are key to building loyalty and trust.

b. Enhanced Engagement:
A well-told story captivates your audience, holding their attention longer than dry, factual content. This increased engagement can lead to higher conversion rates.

c. Memorable Messaging:
People are more likely to remember stories than lists of facts or product features. Stories help your message stick in the minds of your audience.

d. Differentiation:
In a crowded marketplace, storytelling can set your brand apart. It showcases your unique values, culture, and personality, making you stand out from competitors.

e. Influence and Persuasion:

Stories can be persuasive by illustrating real-life examples of how your products or services have made a difference. They help overcome objections and build credibility.

2. Elements of a Compelling Story

a. Relatable Characters:

Your story should feature characters that your audience can relate to. These could be customers, employees, or even the brand itself as a character.

b. Clear Conflict or Challenge:

A compelling story often involves a conflict or challenge that needs to be overcome. This element keeps the audience invested in the outcome.

c. Emotional Arc:

The emotional journey of the characters, including highs and lows, helps to engage the audience on a deeper level. Emotions like joy, fear, surprise, and relief make the story more impactful.

d. Resolution:

A satisfying resolution to the conflict or challenge provides closure and reinforces the message you want to convey. It often highlights the benefits or value of your product or service.

e. Authenticity:

Authentic stories resonate more with audiences. Ensure your story is genuine and reflects real experiences and values.

3. Best Practices for Integrating Storytelling into Your Content Strategy

a. Know Your Audience:
Understand your audience's values, interests, and pain points. Tailor your stories to address these aspects and make them more relatable.

b. Align with Brand Values:
Your stories should reflect your brand's core values and mission. Consistency in messaging reinforces your brand identity and builds trust.

c. Use Various Formats:
Incorporate storytelling across different content formats, such as blog posts, videos, social media updates, podcasts, and case studies. Each format can add a unique dimension to your storytelling.

d. Show, Don't Tell:
Use vivid descriptions, dialogues, and visual elements to show the story rather than just telling it. This makes the story more immersive and engaging.

e. Highlight Customer Stories:
Featuring your customers' success stories can be highly effective. Real-life testimonials and case studies demonstrate the practical benefits of your products or services.

f. Create a Narrative Arc:
Structure your content with a clear beginning, middle, and end. Introduce the characters and setting, present the conflict or challenge, and conclude with the resolution.

g. Leverage Visuals and Multimedia:
Enhance your stories with visuals, such as images, infographics, and videos. Multimedia elements can make the story more engaging and easier to understand.

h. Be Consistent:
Consistency is key in storytelling. Regularly share stories that reinforce your brand message across all channels to build a cohesive narrative.

4. Examples of Effective Storytelling in Marketing

a. Brand Origin Stories:
Share the history and inspiration behind your brand. This can humanize your business and create an emotional connection with your audience.

b. Customer Success Stories:
Highlight how your product or service has positively impacted a customer's life or business. Use detailed narratives and real quotes to add authenticity.

c. Behind-the-Scenes Stories:
Give your audience a glimpse into the people, processes, and values that drive your business. This transparency can build trust and loyalty.

d. Mission-Driven Stories:
Share stories that reflect your brand's mission and values. For example, if you're committed to sustainability, tell stories about your environmental initiatives.

5. Measuring the Impact of Storytelling

a. Engagement Metrics:
Track metrics such as likes, shares, comments, and time spent on page to gauge how well your stories are resonating with your audience.

b. Conversion Rates:
Analyze conversion rates for content pieces that incorporate storytelling. Higher conversion rates can indicate that your stories are effectively influencing decisions.

d. Audience Growth:
Measure the growth of your audience and followers over time. Compelling storytelling can attract new customers and retain existing ones.

WRITING FOR YOUR AUDIENCE

Writing for your audience is a crucial aspect of content creation. Understanding who your audience is and tailoring your content to their needs, preferences, and pain points can significantly enhance engagement, build trust, and drive conversions. This section explores the importance of audience-centric writing, techniques to understand your audience better, and best practices for crafting content that resonates with them.

1. Importance of Audience-Centric Writing

a. Enhances Engagement:
Content that speaks directly to the interests and concerns of your audience is more likely to capture and hold their attention.

b. Builds Trust and Credibility:
Demonstrating an understanding of your audience's needs and providing relevant solutions establishes your brand as a trusted resource.

c. Drives Conversions:
Tailored content can guide your audience through the buyer's journey, addressing their specific questions and objections, and leading to higher conversion rates.

2. Techniques to Understand Your Audience

a. Create Detailed Buyer Personas:
- Develop semi-fictional representations of your ideal customers based on market research and real data.
- Include demographic information, interests, pain points, goals, and preferred communication channels.

b. Conduct Surveys and Interviews:
- Gather direct feedback from your audience through surveys, interviews, and questionnaires.
- Ask about their challenges, preferences, and what type of content they find most valuable.

c. Analyze Website and Social Media Analytics:
- Use tools like Google Analytics and social media insights to understand your audience's behavior and interests.
- Monitor which content types and topics generate the most engagement.

d. Engage in Social Listening:
- Track online conversations about your brand, competitors, and industry.
- Identify common questions, concerns, and trending topics within your audience.

e. Review Customer Feedback:
- Regularly check reviews, comments, and feedback from customers to understand their experiences and expectations.

3. Best Practices for Crafting Audience-Centric Content

a. Use a Conversational Tone:
- Write in a way that feels personal and relatable. Avoid jargon and overly formal language.
- Aim for a conversational tone that makes your content easy to read and engaging.

b. Address Pain Points Directly:
- Identify the common challenges and problems your audience faces.
- Provide solutions, tips, and insights that address these pain points directly in your content.

c. Focus on Benefits, Not Just Features:
- Highlight how your product or service can benefit your audience, rather than just listing its features.
- Explain how it solves their problems or improves their situation.

d. Use Clear and Compelling Headlines:
- Craft headlines that grab attention and clearly convey the value of your content.
- Use action words, numbers, and questions to make headlines more engaging.

e. Incorporate Storytelling:
- Use storytelling techniques to make your content more engaging and memorable.
- Share customer success stories, case studies, or personal anecdotes that resonate with your audience.

f. Include Visuals and Multimedia:
- Enhance your written content with images, videos, infographics, and other multimedia elements.
- Visuals can help illustrate your points and make the content more appealing.

g. Optimize for SEO Without Sacrificing Readability:
- Incorporate relevant keywords naturally within your content to improve search engine rankings.
- Ensure the content remains readable and valuable to human readers, not just search engines.

h. Provide Clear CTAs:

- Guide your audience towards the next step with clear and compelling calls-to-action (CTAs).
- Whether it's downloading a resource, signing up for a newsletter, or making a purchase, make the CTA obvious and easy to follow.

4. Adapting Content for Different Platforms

a. Blog Posts:

- Write detailed, informative posts that provide in-depth insights and solutions.
- Use subheadings, bullet points, and images to break up text and improve readability.

b. Social Media:

- Create concise, attention-grabbing content that encourages interaction and sharing.
- Use visuals and hashtags to increase visibility and engagement.

c. Email Newsletters:

- Personalize your emails with the recipient's name and tailored content.
- Keep the content focused and provide clear CTAs to drive action.

d. Whitepapers and E-books:

- Offer comprehensive, well-researched content that provides significant value.
- Include data, case studies, and detailed analyses to establish authority and credibility.

e. Video Scripts:

- Write engaging scripts that convey your message clearly and concisely.
- Use a conversational tone and incorporate storytelling to maintain viewer interest.

5. Measuring the Effectiveness of Your Content

a. Engagement Metrics:
- Track metrics such as page views, time on page, social shares, and comments to gauge how well your content resonates.
- Monitor click-through rates and conversion rates for content with CTAs.

b. Feedback and Surveys:
- Collect feedback from your audience to understand what they find valuable and where improvements can be made.
- Use surveys to gather insights on content preferences and effectiveness.

c. Analytics Tools:
- Use tools like Google Analytics, social media insights, and email marketing platforms to track performance.
- Analyze data to identify trends and adjust your content strategy accordingly.

THE IMPORTANCE OF HEADLINES & HOOKS

Headlines and hooks play a crucial role in content marketing by capturing your audience's attention and enticing them to engage with your content. They are often the first impression a reader has of your content, and a strong headline paired with an effective hook can significantly increase the likelihood of your content being read, shared, and acted upon.

1. The Importance of Headlines

a. Capturing Attention:
- Headlines are the first thing a reader sees, whether in search results, social media feeds, or email subject lines.
- A compelling headline grabs attention instantly and encourages the reader to click and read further.

b. Setting Expectations:
- A good headline gives a clear indication of what the content is about.
- It sets the tone and provides a preview of the value the reader will receive, helping them decide if it's worth their time.

c. Enhancing SEO:
- Well-crafted headlines with relevant keywords can improve your content's search engine rankings.
- Headlines optimized for SEO can attract more organic traffic to your website.

d. Increasing Shareability:
- Engaging headlines are more likely to be shared on social media, broadening your content's reach.
- They can spark curiosity and encourage readers to share with their networks.

2. The Importance of Hooks

a. Engaging the Reader:
- A strong hook in the opening sentence or paragraph pulls the reader into the content.
- It piques curiosity and encourages the reader to continue reading.

b. Building Interest:
- Hooks create an emotional or intellectual connection with the reader, making them want to learn more.
- They can introduce an intriguing fact, a compelling question, or a bold statement that resonates with the audience.

c. Encouraging Action:
- Effective hooks can motivate readers to take action, whether it's reading further, sharing the content, or clicking on a CTA.
- They help in building momentum and maintaining engagement throughout the content.

3. Elements of Effective Headlines

a. Clarity:
- Clear and concise headlines communicate the main idea without ambiguity.
- Avoid jargon and complex language that might confuse the reader.

b. Relevance:
- Ensure the headline is relevant to the target audience's interests and needs.
- It should address a specific problem, question, or topic of interest to the reader.

c. Specificity:
- Specific headlines provide precise information about what the reader can expect.
- Use numbers, dates, and specific details to make the headline more informative and enticing.

d. Emotional Appeal:
- Headlines that evoke emotions, such as curiosity, excitement, or urgency, are more compelling.
- Use powerful words and phrases that resonate emotionally with the reader.

e. Keywords:
- Incorporate relevant keywords naturally to improve SEO and attract the right audience.
- Avoid keyword stuffing, which can make the headline awkward or spammy.

4. Elements of Effective Hooks

a. Intriguing Questions:
- Start with a question that makes the reader think and want to find the answer.
- Ensure the question is relevant and thought-provoking.

b. Surprising Facts:
  - Share a surprising or little-known fact that grabs attention.
  - Ensure the fact is interesting and directly related to the content.

c. Bold Statements:
  - Use bold or controversial statements to create interest and curiosity.
  - Make sure the statement is supported by the content and not just clickbait.

d. Anecdotes and Stories:
  - Begin with a short, engaging story or anecdote that draws the reader in.
  - Relate the story to the main topic to maintain relevance.

e. Promises and Benefits:
  - Highlight the main benefit or value the reader will gain from the content.
  - Make a promise that addresses the reader's needs or pain points.

5. Best Practices for Crafting Headlines and Hooks

a. A/B Testing:
  - Test different headlines and hooks to see which ones resonate best with your audience.
  - Use analytics tools to track performance and refine your approach based on data.

b. Keep It Short and Sweet:
  - Aim for headlines that are concise, ideally between 6-12 words.
  - Hooks should be brief enough to capture interest quickly but detailed enough to draw the reader in.

c. Focus on the Reader:
- Write from the reader's perspective, addressing their interests and concerns.
- Use "you" and "your" to make the content feel more personal and engaging.

d. Use Action Words:
- Start headlines and hooks with strong action words that encourage readers to take immediate action.
- Words like "discover," "learn," "find out," and "explore" can make your content more dynamic.

e. Revise and Refine:
- Don't settle for the first headline or hook you come up with. Brainstorm multiple options and refine them.
- Seek feedback from colleagues or conduct informal surveys to choose the most effective ones.

6. Examples of Effective Headlines and Hooks

Headlines:
- "10 Proven Strategies to Boost Your Website Traffic"
- "How to Save Money on Your Energy Bills: Tips from Experts"
- "The Ultimate Guide to Social Media Marketing for Beginners"
- "Unlock the Secrets of a Successful Startup: Insider Tips"

Hooks:
- "Did you know that businesses with blogs generate 67% more leads than those without? Let's explore how you can harness this power."
- "Imagine doubling your website traffic in just 30 days. Here's how one small change can make a big difference."
- "Ever wondered why some startups succeed while others fail? It all comes down to these key factors."
- "Struggling to save on your energy bills? You're not alone, but these expert tips can help you make significant savings."

BEST PRACTICES FOR SEO CONTENT

Search Engine Optimization (SEO) is a critical component of content marketing. By optimizing your content for search engines, you can improve your website's visibility, drive organic traffic, and enhance user engagement. SEO practices evolve constantly, and staying updated with the latest trends and algorithms is essential.

1. Understand Search Intent

a. Types of Search Intent:
   - Informational: Users looking for information on a specific topic.
   - Navigational: Users searching for a particular website or page.
   - Transactional: Users intending to make a purchase or complete an action.
   - Commercial Investigation: Users researching products or services before making a purchase decision.

b. Align Content with Intent:
   - Create content that matches the search intent of your target audience.
   - Use keyword research tools to understand what users are searching for and the intent behind those searches.

2. Optimize for Featured Snippets and Rich Results

a. Featured Snippets:
   - Answer common questions directly within your content.
   - Use clear and concise formatting, such as bullet points, numbered lists, and tables.
   - Include the question as a header (H2 or H3) followed by a brief, direct answer.

b. Rich Results:
- Use structured data (schema markup) to help search engines understand your content.
- Implement schema types such as FAQs, how-tos, reviews, and recipes to enhance your listings.

3. Focus on E-A-T (Expertise, Authoritativeness, Trustworthiness)

a. Expertise:
- Ensure your content is accurate, well-researched, and written by knowledgeable authors.
- Highlight the credentials of the content creators where applicable.

b. Authoritativeness:
- Build backlinks from reputable websites to boost your domain authority.
- Get mentioned or cited by industry experts and authoritative sources.

c. Trustworthiness:
- Maintain a professional website design and user experience.
- Provide clear contact information and privacy policies.
- Encourage customer reviews and testimonials to build trust.

4. Enhance User Experience (UX)

a. Mobile Optimization:
- Ensure your website is mobile-friendly and responsive.
- Use Google's Mobile-Friendly Test tool to check your site's compatibility.

b. Page Speed:
- Optimize images, enable browser caching, and minimize JavaScript to improve load times.
- Use tools like Google PageSpeed Insights to identify and fix performance issues.

c. Easy Navigation:
- Design a clear and intuitive navigation structure.
- Use breadcrumbs to help users and search engines understand your site's hierarchy.

5. Keyword Research and Optimization

a. Long-Tail Keywords:
- Target long-tail keywords that are specific and less competitive.
- Use tools like Google Keyword Planner, Ahrefs, or SEMrush to find relevant long-tail keywords.

b. Keyword Placement:
- Incorporate primary keywords naturally in the title, headings, URL, and throughout the content.
- Avoid keyword stuffing; prioritize readability and user experience.

c. Latent Semantic Indexing (LSI) Keywords:
- Use LSI keywords to provide context and relevance to your content.
- These are related terms and phrases that help search engines understand the topic better.

6. Create High-Quality, Engaging Content

a. Content Depth:
- Aim for comprehensive content that covers topics thoroughly.
- Use supporting visuals, examples, and data to enrich the content.

b. Readability:
- Write in clear, concise language.
- Use subheadings, bullet points, and short paragraphs to improve readability.

c. Multimedia Integration:
   - Include images, videos, infographics, and other multimedia elements to enhance engagement.
   - Optimize all multimedia for SEO by using descriptive file names and alt text.

7. Regularly Update and Repurpose Content

a. Content Updates:
   - Regularly review and update older content to keep it relevant and accurate.
   - Add new information, update statistics, and refresh visuals as needed.

b. Content Repurposing:
   - Repurpose existing content into different formats, such as turning blog posts into videos or infographics.
   - Share repurposed content across various platforms to reach a broader audience.

8. Optimize Meta Tags and Descriptions

a. Title Tags:
   - Craft unique, descriptive, and compelling title tags for each page.
   - Keep titles under 60 characters to ensure they display fully in search results.

b. Meta Descriptions:
   - Write concise meta descriptions (150-160 characters) that summarize the page content and include a call-to-action.
   - Use primary keywords naturally within the meta description.

9. Leverage Internal and External Linking

a. Internal Linking:
- Link to relevant content within your website to guide users and distribute link equity.
- Use descriptive anchor text that indicates the linked content's topic.

b. External Linking:
- Link to authoritative and relevant external websites to provide additional value and context.
- Ensure that external links open in a new tab to keep users on your site.

10. Monitor and Analyze Performance

a. SEO Tools:
- Use tools like Google Analytics, Google Search Console, Ahrefs, and SEMrush to monitor your SEO performance.
- Track key metrics such as organic traffic, bounce rates, conversion rates, and keyword rankings.

b. Regular Audits:
- Conduct regular SEO audits to identify and fix issues that may impact your site's performance.
- Stay updated with the latest SEO trends and algorithm changes to adjust your strategy accordingly.

CHAPTER 5

Video Marketing Essentials

Video marketing has become a dominant force in the digital marketing landscape, transforming the way brands communicate with their audiences. This shift is driven by the growing preference for video content among consumers and the effectiveness of video in delivering engaging, memorable, and persuasive messages. This section explores the rise of video marketing, its benefits, and why it has become essential for businesses of all sizes.

Video content consumption has skyrocketed in recent years, with platforms like YouTube, TikTok, Instagram, and Facebook leading the charge. According to recent studies, **over 85% of internet users in the U.S. watch online video content monthly across various devices.**

The proliferation of smartphones and high-speed internet has significantly contributed to the rise of mobile video consumption. Short-form video content, in particular, has thrived on mobile platforms, catering to on-the-go viewers looking for quick, engaging content. **The growth of platforms like TikTok, Instagram Reels, and YouTube Shorts has introduced new formats and opportunities for video marketing.** Live streaming on platforms such as Facebook Live, Instagram Live, and Twitch has also gained popularity, offering real-time interaction with audiences.

BENEFITS OF VIDEO CONTENT

Video content has become an indispensable part of modern marketing strategies, offering numerous advantages that can significantly enhance a brand's engagement, reach, and conversion rates.

1. Enhanced Engagement

a. Capturing Attention:

- Videos combine visuals, sound, and motion to create a multi-sensory experience that captures attention more effectively than text or static images.
- Engaging thumbnails and dynamic content can attract viewers and keep them interested longer.

b. Increased Interaction:

- Video content encourages interaction through comments, likes, shares, and subscriptions, fostering a sense of community and dialogue.
- Platforms like YouTube and social media sites provide features that make it easy for viewers to engage with videos.

2. Improved Conversion Rates

a. Demonstrating Value:

- Videos can effectively showcase the benefits and features of products or services, making it easier for potential customers to understand their value.
- Demonstrations and explainer videos help bridge the gap between curiosity and purchase decision.

b. Building Trust and Credibility:

- Customer testimonials, case studies, and behind-the-scenes videos build trust by showing real people and genuine experiences.
- Authentic content helps to humanize your brand and establish credibility.

c. Stronger Call-to-Action (CTA):

- Videos can incorporate clear and compelling CTAs, guiding viewers towards desired actions such as subscribing, visiting a website, or making a purchase.
- End screens and interactive elements can further enhance the effectiveness of CTAs.

3. Better Information Retention

a. Visual and Auditory Learning:

- Videos cater to both visual and auditory learners, making it easier for viewers to absorb and retain information.
- Animated graphics, charts, and visuals can simplify complex information and improve comprehension.

b. Storytelling:

- Videos are an excellent medium for storytelling, allowing brands to convey messages in a more engaging and memorable way.
- Emotional storytelling can create a lasting impact and help in building a stronger connection with the audience.

4. Boosted SEO and Online Visibility

a. Higher Rankings:

- Search engines favor websites with diverse and engaging content, including videos, which can improve your SEO rankings.
- Videos can appear in search results and increase the visibility of your website.

b. Increased Dwell Time:

- Videos can increase the amount of time visitors spend on your website, signaling to search engines that your site provides valuable content.
- Longer dwell times can positively impact your SEO performance.

c. Rich Snippets and Thumbnails:
   - Video content can generate rich snippets and attractive thumbnails in search results, making your listings more appealing and clickable.

5. Expanded Reach on Social Media

a. Algorithm Favoritism:
   - Social media algorithms prioritize video content, increasing the likelihood that your videos will be seen by a larger audience.
   - Videos often receive higher engagement rates compared to other types of content.

b. Shareability:
   - Videos are highly shareable, allowing your content to reach a wider audience organically.
   - Compelling and entertaining videos can go viral, significantly amplifying your brand's reach.

6. Versatility and Flexibility

a. Multiple Formats:
   - Videos can be repurposed across different platforms and formats, such as social media clips, blog embeds, email marketing, and webinars.
   - This versatility ensures that your content reaches various segments of your audience in the most effective manner.

b. Various Uses:
   - Videos can serve multiple purposes, from brand awareness and education to lead generation and customer support.
   - Different types of videos, such as tutorials, interviews, product reviews, and event coverage, cater to different marketing objectives.

7. Enhanced Emotional Connection

a. Personal Touch:
- Videos can convey personality and emotion, helping to create a personal connection between the brand and its audience.
- Facial expressions, tone of voice, and storytelling elements can evoke emotions and foster empathy.

b. Relatability:
- Content featuring real people, such as employees, customers, or influencers, makes your brand more relatable and trustworthy.
- Viewers are more likely to connect with and remember content that feels personal and authentic.

8. Increased Accessibility

a. Mobile Compatibility:
- Videos are easily consumable on mobile devices, making them accessible to users on the go.
- Short-form videos, in particular, are ideal for mobile viewing and can capture attention quickly.

b. Accessibility Features:
- Adding subtitles and captions to videos makes them accessible to a wider audience, including those with hearing impairments or language barriers.
- Descriptive audio and visual cues can enhance accessibility for visually impaired viewers.

9. Higher Engagement with Email Campaigns

a. Improved Open Rates:
- Including the word "video" in email subject lines can increase open rates, as it signals valuable and engaging content.
- Videos in emails can capture attention and entice recipients to click through.

b. Enhanced Click-Through Rates:
- Embedding videos or including video thumbnails in emails can boost click-through rates, driving more traffic to your website or landing pages.
- Engaging video content can enhance the overall effectiveness of your email marketing campaigns.

TYPES OF VIDEO CONTENT

Video content comes in various formats, each serving different purposes and appealing to different audience preferences. Understanding the types of video content and how to use them effectively can enhance your marketing strategy and help you achieve your business goals.

1. Explainer Videos

a. Definition:
- Short videos that explain a product, service, or concept in a simple and engaging manner.
- Typically 1-3 minutes long.

b. Benefits:
- Simplify complex information.
- Enhance understanding and retention.
- Drive conversions by clearly explaining value propositions.

c. Best Practices:
- Use clear and concise language.
- Incorporate visuals and animations to illustrate key points.
- Focus on the problem-solution framework.

2. Product Demos

a. Definition:
- Videos that showcase the features and benefits of a product, demonstrating how it works.
- Can range from short clips to detailed walkthroughs.

b. Benefits:
  - Allow potential customers to see the product in action.
  - Highlight key features and benefits.
  - Build trust and credibility.

c. Best Practices:
  - Show the product in use, focusing on its main features.
  - Include close-ups and detailed shots.
  - Use real-life scenarios to demonstrate value.

3. Customer Testimonials

a. Definition:
  - Videos featuring satisfied customers sharing their positive experiences with your brand.
  - Typically 1-2 minutes long.

b. Benefits:
  - Build trust and social proof.
  - Provide authentic and relatable endorsements.
  - Address potential objections and concerns.

c. Best Practices:
  - Select genuine and enthusiastic customers.
  - Focus on specific benefits and outcomes.
  - Keep the testimonials authentic and unscripted.

4. Behind-the-Scenes Videos

a. Definition:
  - Videos that give viewers a glimpse into the inner workings of your company.
  - Can cover various aspects such as office tours, team introductions, and production processes.

b. Benefits:
  - Humanize your brand.
  - Build a deeper connection with your audience.
  - Showcase company culture and values.

c. Best Practices:
- Highlight interesting and unique aspects of your business.
- Keep the tone casual and personable.
- Use interviews and candid shots to add authenticity.

5. Educational Videos

a. Definition:
- Informative videos that provide valuable information, tips, and tutorials related to your industry.
- Can vary in length depending on the depth of the topic.

b. Benefits:
- Establish your brand as an authority.
- Provide value to your audience, fostering loyalty.
- Attract organic traffic through search queries.

c. Best Practices:
- Focus on topics relevant to your audience's needs.
- Use clear and structured explanations.
- Incorporate visuals and examples to enhance understanding.

6. Live Videos

a. Definition:
- Real-time video broadcasts that allow for immediate interaction with viewers.
- Common platforms include Facebook Live, Instagram Live, and YouTube Live.

b. Benefits:
- Foster real-time engagement and interaction.
- Create a sense of urgency and exclusivity.
- Allow for spontaneous and authentic communication.

c. Best Practices:
   - Promote the live event in advance to build anticipation.
   - Engage with viewers by responding to comments and questions.
   - Keep the session interactive and dynamic.

7. Social Media Clips

a. Definition:
   - Short, engaging videos designed for social media platforms like Instagram, Facebook, and TikTok.
   - Typically under 60 seconds.

b. Benefits:
   - Capture attention quickly in busy social feeds.
   - Encourage sharing and viral potential.
   - Drive traffic and engagement on social platforms.

c. Best Practices:
   - Use eye-catching visuals and strong hooks.
   - Keep the message clear and concise.
   - Leverage trending topics and hashtags.

8. Webinars

a. Definition:
   - Online seminars or workshops that provide in-depth information on a specific topic.
   - Typically 30 minutes to an hour long.

b. Benefits:
   - Offer valuable insights and education to your audience.
   - Allow for direct interaction through Q&A sessions.
   - Position your brand as a thought leader.

c. Best Practices:
- Choose relevant and timely topics.
- Use engaging visuals and interactive elements.
- Promote the webinar through various channels to attract attendees.

9. Animation and Motion Graphics

a. Definition:
- Videos that use animated graphics and illustrations to convey messages.
- Can be used for explainer videos, ads, and educational content.

b. Benefits:
- Simplify complex concepts through visual storytelling.
- Capture attention with creative and dynamic visuals.
- Offer flexibility in style and design.

c. Best Practices:
- Use professional animation tools and techniques.
- Ensure the visuals align with your brand identity.
- Focus on clarity and simplicity.

10. Vlogs

a. Definition:
- Video blogs that provide a personal perspective on topics related to your brand or industry.
- Can be informal and conversational in tone.

b. Benefits:
- Build a personal connection with your audience.
- Showcase your expertise and personality.
- Foster a loyal community of viewers.

c. Best Practices:
- Maintain a consistent posting schedule.
- Engage with viewers through comments and feedback.
- Keep the content authentic and relatable.

CHOOSING THE RIGHT FORMAT AND LENGTH FOR YOUR VIDEOS

Selecting the appropriate format and length for your videos is crucial to maximizing their effectiveness and ensuring they resonate with your audience. Different types of content and platforms require varying approaches to video length and format.

1. Understanding Your Audience and Goals

a. Audience Preferences:
- Identify your target audience and understand their content consumption habits.
- Consider factors such as age, interests, and preferred social media platforms.

b. Marketing Goals:
- Define the primary objective of your video (e.g., brand awareness, lead generation, education, sales).
- Align the format and length with your specific goals to ensure maximum impact.

2. Short-Form vs. Long-Form Videos

a. Short-Form Videos:
- Duration: Typically under 60 seconds, often between 15 to 30 seconds.
- Platforms: Ideal for social media platforms like TikTok, Instagram Reels, YouTube Shorts, and Facebook Stories.
- Purpose: Capturing attention quickly, driving engagement, and promoting shareability.

b. Long-Form Videos:

   - Duration: Generally longer than 2 minutes, can range from 5 to 30 minutes or more.
   - Platforms: Best suited for YouTube, Vimeo, webinars, and video courses.
   - Purpose: Providing in-depth information, detailed tutorials, and comprehensive storytelling.

3. Choosing the Right Video Format

a. Explainer Videos:

   - Format: Typically short-form, between 1 to 3 minutes.
   - Purpose: Explain a concept, product, or service in a clear and engaging manner.
   - Best Practices: Use animations, voiceovers, and straightforward language.

b. Product Demos:

   - Format: Can be both short-form (teasers) and long-form (detailed demos).
   - Purpose: Showcase product features, benefits, and usage.
   - Best Practices: Highlight key features, use high-quality visuals, and include a clear CTA.

c. Customer Testimonials:

   - Format: Usually short-form, around 1 to 2 minutes.
   - Purpose: Build trust and credibility through real customer experiences.
   - Best Practices: Keep it authentic, focus on specific benefits, and use real customers.

d. Educational Videos:

   - Format: Generally long-form, ranging from 5 to 20 minutes or more.
   - Purpose: Provide valuable information, tips, and tutorials.
   - Best Practices: Break down complex topics, use visuals and examples, and maintain a structured format.

e. Social Media Clips:
   - Format: Short-form, typically under 60 seconds.
   - Purpose: Capture attention quickly and drive engagement on social platforms.
   - Best Practices: Use eye-catching visuals, strong hooks, and relevant hashtags.

f. Live Videos:
   - Format: Can vary, usually 10 minutes to an hour.
   - Purpose: Real-time interaction and engagement with viewers.
   - Best Practices: Promote the event in advance, engage with comments, and maintain a dynamic flow.

g. Behind-the-Scenes Videos:
   - Format: Can be both short-form and long-form, depending on content depth.
   - Purpose: Showcase company culture, processes, and people.
   - Best Practices: Keep it informal, use candid shots, and tell a story.

h. Vlogs:
   - Format: Typically long-form, 5 to 15 minutes.
   - Purpose: Provide personal insights, experiences, and commentary.
   - Best Practices: Be consistent, engage with viewers, and keep it authentic.

i. Webinars:
   - Format: Long-form, usually 30 minutes to an hour.
   - Purpose: Deliver in-depth information and interact with a live audience.
   - Best Practices: Plan a clear agenda, use interactive elements, and follow up with attendees.

4. Platform-Specific Considerations

a. YouTube:
- Ideal for both short-form and long-form content.
- Optimize titles, descriptions, and tags for SEO.
- Use engaging thumbnails and end screens.

b. Instagram:
- Use Reels for short, engaging clips.
- Stories for ephemeral content that lasts 24 hours.

c. TikTok:
- Focus on very short-form content, typically 15 to 60 seconds.
- Leverage trends, music, and effects to increase visibility.

d. Facebook:
- Use short-form videos for feeds and stories.
- Longer videos for Facebook Watch and live streams.

e. LinkedIn:
- Short, professional videos for updates and company news.
- Longer videos for webinars and thought leadership content.

5. Testing and Optimization

a. A/B Testing:
- Test different video lengths and formats to see which performs best with your audience.
- Use metrics like watch time, engagement, and conversion rates to determine effectiveness.

b. Analyze Performance:
- Regularly review video analytics to understand viewer behavior and preferences.
- Adjust your strategy based on insights to improve future videos.

c. Continuous Improvement:

- Keep up with trends and platform updates to ensure your video content remains relevant.
- Experiment with new formats and styles to keep your audience engaged.

YouTube Marketing

WHY YOUTUBE IS CRUCIAL FOR VIDEO MARKETING

YouTube has firmly established itself as a cornerstone of digital marketing, offering unparalleled opportunities for brands to reach and engage with a global audience. **As the second most visited website in the world and the second largest search engine after Google, YouTube boasts over 2 billion logged-in monthly users.** This vast user base provides an immense potential audience for businesses, making YouTube an essential platform for any comprehensive video marketing strategy.

One of the primary reasons YouTube is crucial for video marketing is its ability to enhance brand visibility and reach. The platform's extensive global audience allows brands to connect with diverse demographics, expanding their market presence. **YouTube's search and recommendation algorithms are designed to promote relevant content, increasing the likelihood that videos will reach interested viewers.** This capability helps brands attract not only a broad audience but also a targeted one, ensuring that marketing efforts are more effective and efficient.

YouTube also excels in driving organic traffic and improving search engine optimization (SEO). Videos on YouTube are indexed by Google, meaning that a well-optimized YouTube channel can significantly boost a brand's visibility in search engine results pages (SERPs). By incorporating relevant keywords in video titles, descriptions, and tags, brands can improve their SEO performance, making it easier for potential customers to discover their content. Furthermore, YouTube's integration with other social media platforms allows for seamless sharing and embedding, further amplifying a video's reach and impact.

CHAPTER 6 YouTube Marketing

Engagement is another critical factor that underscores the importance of YouTube in video marketing. Video content is inherently more engaging than text or static images, and YouTube provides numerous features that enhance viewer interaction. **Comments, likes, shares, and subscriptions enable brands to build a community around their content, fostering loyalty and encouraging ongoing engagement.** Additionally, YouTube's live streaming capabilities offer real-time interaction with audiences, providing opportunities for immediate feedback and more personal connections with viewers.

Monetization opportunities on YouTube add another layer of value for brands. **Through the YouTube Partner Program, creators can earn revenue from ads displayed on their videos.** This monetization potential incentivizes the production of high-quality content and provides an additional revenue stream for businesses. Moreover, **brands can leverage YouTube's advertising platform to run targeted ad campaigns,** reaching specific audiences based on demographics, interests, and behavior. This dual approach of earning ad revenue and utilizing paid advertising makes YouTube a versatile tool for both organic and paid marketing efforts.

Furthermore, YouTube's analytics and insights offer valuable data that can inform and refine marketing strategies. **Detailed metrics on views, watch time, audience demographics, and engagement rates provide a comprehensive understanding of how content is performing and how audiences are interacting with it.** This data-driven approach allows brands to optimize their content, tailoring future videos to better meet the needs and preferences of their audience.

SETTING UP AND OPTIMIZING YOUR YOUTUBE CHANNEL

Creating a successful YouTube channel requires more than just uploading videos. To truly leverage the platform's potential, you need to set up and optimize your channel effectively.

1. Setting Up Your YouTube Channel

a. Create a Google Account:
   - Your YouTube channel is linked to a Google account. If you don't have one, create a new Google account specifically for your brand to keep everything organized.

b. Set Up Your Channel:
   - Go to YouTube and sign in with your Google account. Click on your profile picture and select "Your Channel."
   - Choose "Create a Channel" and follow the prompts to set up your channel name and details.

c. Brand Your Channel:
   - Use a consistent brand name, logo, and color scheme to create a cohesive and recognizable presence.
   - Upload a high-quality profile picture and channel banner that reflect your brand identity. The recommended size for channel art is 2560x1440 pixels.

2. Optimizing Your Channel

a. Complete Your Profile:
   - Write a compelling channel description that clearly explains what your channel is about and what viewers can expect. Include relevant keywords to enhance discoverability.
   - Add links to your website, social media profiles, and other relevant platforms in your channel description and on the banner.

b. Create a Channel Trailer:

- A channel trailer is a short video that introduces new visitors to your content. Keep it under a minute and highlight what makes your channel unique.
- Include a strong call-to-action (CTA) encouraging viewers to subscribe.

c. Organize Your Content with Playlists:

- Group related videos into playlists to help viewers find content more easily and keep them engaged longer. Playlists can also rank in search results, providing another opportunity for visibility.
- Create descriptive titles and descriptions for your playlists, incorporating relevant keywords.

d. Customize Your Channel Layout:

- Use the "Customize Channel" option to organize your channel homepage. Feature your best content and playlists in sections to guide visitors through your content.
- Utilize the "Featured Channels" and "Related Channels" sections to recommend other channels and build a community.

3. Pro Tips and Tricks for Optimization

a. Keyword Research and Implementation:

- Conduct thorough keyword research to identify terms your target audience is searching for. Use tools like Google Keyword Planner, Ahrefs, and TubeBuddy.
- Incorporate these keywords naturally in your video titles, descriptions, and tags to improve search rankings.

b. Craft Compelling Thumbnails:

- Create eye-catching thumbnails that accurately represent your content. Use bright colors, readable text, and high-quality images.
- Consistent branding in thumbnails helps viewers recognize your content instantly.

c. Optimize Video Titles and Descriptions:

- Write clear, concise, and keyword-rich titles. Aim for a length of 60 characters or less.
- In the video description, include a brief overview of the content, relevant links, and a CTA. Use up to 5000 characters but focus on the first 150 characters, as they appear above the fold.

d. Use Tags Wisely:

- Add a mix of broad and specific tags to help YouTube understand the context of your videos. Include primary keywords, related terms, and variations.
- Avoid overloading your video with too many tags; focus on relevance.

e. Engage with Your Audience:

- Respond to comments and questions to build a community and encourage engagement. Ask questions in your videos to prompt comments.
- Use YouTube's Community tab to post updates, polls, and interact with your audience outside of video content.

f. Analyze and Adjust:

- Regularly review YouTube Analytics to track performance metrics like watch time, audience retention, and traffic sources.
- Use this data to refine your content strategy, identify what resonates with your audience, and make necessary adjustments.

g. Collaborate with Other Creators:

- Partnering with other YouTubers can help you reach new audiences and grow your subscriber base. Choose collaborators whose content complements yours.
- Cross-promote each other's channels and create joint content that provides value to both audiences.

h. Promote Your Channel:

- Share your videos on social media, embed them in blog posts, and include them in email newsletters to drive traffic to your channel.
- Utilize YouTube ads to reach a broader audience and increase visibility.

i. Maintain a Consistent Posting Schedule:

- Consistency is key to building and retaining an audience. Create a content calendar and stick to a regular upload schedule.
- Inform your audience about your posting schedule in your channel trailer and descriptions.

CONTENT IDEAS AND CREATION TIPS

1. Content Ideas for Your YouTube Channel

a. Tutorials and How-To Videos:

- Create step-by-step guides that teach your audience how to perform specific tasks or use your products effectively.
- These videos are highly searchable and can position you as an expert in your field.

b. Product Reviews and Unboxings:

- Review your products or services, or those relevant to your industry.
- Unboxing videos generate excitement and give potential customers a closer look at what they can expect.

c. Behind-the-Scenes Content:

- Show the human side of your brand by giving viewers a glimpse behind the scenes.
- This can include office tours, day-in-the-life videos, and team introductions.

d. Customer Testimonials and Case Studies:
- Feature satisfied customers sharing their positive experiences with your products or services.
- Highlight specific results and benefits that your audience can relate to.

e. Industry News and Updates:
- Keep your audience informed about the latest trends, news, and developments in your industry.
- Offer your insights and opinions to establish your brand as a thought leader.

f. Q&A Sessions:
- Answer common questions from your audience in a video format.
- This can be a regular series where you address FAQs and provide valuable information.

g. Live Streams:
- Host live events such as webinars, product launches, and Q&A sessions.
- Engage with your audience in real-time and build a stronger community connection.

h. Top Tips and Best Practices:
- Share your top tips and best practices related to your industry or niche.
- These can be quick, actionable insights that provide immediate value to your viewers.

i. Collaborations with Influencers:
- Partner with influencers or other YouTubers in your niche to create collaborative content.
- This can help you reach new audiences and add credibility to your brand.

j. User-Generated Content:
   - Encourage your customers to create videos featuring your products and share their experiences.
   - Showcase these videos on your channel to build trust and community.

2. Creation Tips for High-Quality Videos

a. Plan Your Content:
   - Outline your video content before you start filming.
   - Create a script or bullet points to ensure your video has a clear structure and flows smoothly.

b. Invest in Good Equipment:
   - Use a high-quality camera, microphone, and lighting to enhance the production value of your videos.
   - Even a smartphone with good resolution and additional accessories can produce great results.

c. Optimize Your Setting:
   - Choose a clean, well-lit environment for filming.
   - Pay attention to background noise and visual distractions to ensure a professional appearance.

d. Pay Attention to Audio Quality:
   - Clear audio is crucial for viewer retention.
   - Use a good microphone and minimize background noise to ensure your voice is heard clearly.

e. Edit Your Videos Professionally:
   - Use video editing software to trim unnecessary parts, add transitions, and incorporate text overlays.
   - Include background music, sound effects, and graphics to make your videos more engaging.

f. Add Captions and Subtitles:
- Including captions and subtitles makes your content more accessible and can improve viewer retention.
- It also helps with SEO by providing additional text for search engines to crawl.

g. Engage Your Audience:
- Encourage viewers to like, comment, and subscribe at the beginning and end of your videos.
- Ask questions and invite feedback to foster interaction and build a community.

h. Use Eye-Catching Thumbnails:
- Create custom thumbnails that are visually appealing and accurately represent your video content.
- Thumbnails should include compelling images and text to entice viewers to click.

i. Optimize Video Titles and Descriptions:
- Use relevant keywords in your video titles and descriptions to improve searchability.
- Write clear, concise titles and provide detailed descriptions with links to related content or your website.

j. Monitor Analytics and Feedback:
- Regularly check YouTube Analytics to track the performance of your videos.
- Pay attention to viewer feedback and make adjustments based on what your audience likes and dislikes.

YOUTUBE SEO AND ALGORITHMS

Understanding YouTube SEO and the platform's algorithms is essential for optimizing your videos and channel to achieve higher visibility and engagement. YouTube's search and recommendation algorithms are continually evolving, and staying updated with the latest best practices is crucial for success in 2024.

1. Understanding YouTube's Algorithm

YouTube's algorithm plays a critical role in determining which videos are recommended to users and which ones appear in search results. The algorithm is designed to maximize viewer satisfaction and engagement by showing content that is relevant and likely to be enjoyed.

a. Search Algorithm:
   - YouTube's search algorithm prioritizes relevance, ensuring that the results closely match the user's search query.
   - It considers factors such as the keywords in the video title, description, tags, and the content itself.

b. Recommendation Algorithm:
   - The recommendation algorithm suggests videos on the user's homepage and in the "Up Next" section.
   - It analyzes user behavior, such as watch history, search history, and engagement metrics, to suggest videos that match the user's interests.

2. Key YouTube SEO Strategies for 2024

a. Keyword Research:
   - Conduct thorough keyword research to understand what your target audience is searching for.
   - Use tools like Google Keyword Planner, Ahrefs, and TubeBuddy to identify relevant keywords and phrases.
   - Incorporate these keywords naturally in your video titles, descriptions, tags, and transcripts.

b. Optimizing Titles and Descriptions:
- Create compelling and descriptive titles that include primary keywords. Aim for clarity and relevance within 60 characters to ensure the title is fully displayed.
- Write detailed descriptions that provide context, include keywords, and add links to your website and social media profiles. The first 150 characters are crucial as they appear above the fold.

c. Utilizing Tags Effectively:
- Use a mix of broad and specific tags to help YouTube understand the context of your video.
- Include primary keywords, related terms, and variations to improve searchability.

d. Creating Engaging Thumbnails:
- Design custom thumbnails that are eye-catching and relevant to your video content.
- Use bright colors, readable text, and high-quality images to attract clicks.
- Consistent branding in thumbnails helps with channel recognition and user engagement.

e. Captions and Transcripts:
- Adding accurate captions and transcripts can improve accessibility and SEO.
- Captions help in capturing a broader audience, including those who watch videos without sound.

f. Encouraging Engagement:
- Foster viewer engagement by asking questions, prompting likes, comments, and subscriptions.
- Higher engagement signals to YouTube that your content is valuable, potentially boosting its visibility.

g. Leveraging Playlists:

- Organize your videos into playlists based on themes or series.
- Playlists can improve watch time and keep viewers on your channel longer.
- Each playlist should have a clear title and description with relevant keywords.

h. Promoting Videos:

- Share your videos across social media, embed them in blog posts, and include them in email newsletters.
- Cross-promotion increases visibility and can drive more traffic to your channel.

3. Insights into YouTube's 2024 Algorithm Changes

a. Enhanced User Behavior Analysis:

- The algorithm is becoming more sophisticated in analyzing user behavior patterns, such as watch time, session duration, and interaction history.
- Focus on creating content that encourages viewers to watch longer and engage more.

b. Emphasis on Quality Content:

- YouTube prioritizes high-quality content that provides value to viewers. This includes educational content, detailed tutorials, and well-produced videos.
- Regularly updating and improving your content can help maintain its relevance and ranking.

c. Personalization and Viewer Satisfaction:

- The algorithm now places greater emphasis on personalized recommendations, aiming to increase viewer satisfaction.
- Tailor your content to your audience's preferences by analyzing viewer demographics and feedback.

d. Mobile Optimization:

- With a significant portion of users accessing YouTube via mobile devices, the algorithm favors content optimized for mobile viewing.
- Ensure your videos are mobile-friendly, with clear visuals and readable text.

4. Tools and Resources for YouTube SEO

a. YouTube Analytics:

- Use YouTube Analytics to monitor performance metrics such as views, watch time, audience retention, and engagement.
- Analyze this data to understand what works and refine your strategy accordingly.

b. SEO Tools:

- Tools like TubeBuddy, VidIQ, and Ahrefs can provide valuable insights into keyword performance, competitor analysis, and SEO optimization tips.
- Use these tools to optimize your videos and track your SEO progress.

c. Social Media Listening:

- Use social media listening tools to understand trending topics and audience sentiments.
- Incorporate these insights into your content planning to stay relevant and engaging.

TikTok Marketing

THE RISE OF TIKTOK AND ITS UNIQUE AUDIENCE

In recent years, **TikTok has emerged as a powerhouse in the social media landscape, captivating millions of users worldwide with its unique blend of creativity, entertainment, and community engagement.** Since its launch in 2016, TikTok has grown exponentially, boasting **over a billion active users as of 2024.** This rapid rise can be attributed to its distinct format, user-friendly interface, and the ability to create and share short, engaging videos with a global audience. For marketers, understanding the rise of TikTok and its unique audience is crucial for leveraging the platform effectively.

One of the primary factors behind TikTok's meteoric rise is its appeal to younger demographics. The platform is particularly popular among Generation Z and Millennials, with a significant portion of its user base being under the age of 30. This youthful audience is drawn to TikTok's **dynamic and interactive nature**, where they can express themselves creatively through a variety of video formats, including lip-syncing, dancing, comedy sketches, and educational content. The app's algorithm, which promotes content based on user interactions rather than follower counts, allows new creators to gain visibility quickly, fostering a sense of inclusivity and community.

CHAPTER 7   TikTok Marketing

TikTok's unique audience is characterized by its appetite for authentic and relatable content. Unlike other social media platforms that often emphasize polished and curated posts, **TikTok thrives on spontaneity and rawness.** Users appreciate content that feels genuine and unfiltered, making it easier for brands to connect with their audience on a more personal level. **This preference for authenticity has led to the rise of influencers who are not necessarily celebrities but ordinary people with compelling stories or talents.** For brands, collaborating with these influencers can be an effective way to reach and engage with their target audience.

Another defining feature of TikTok's audience is its high level of engagement. **TikTok users are not just passive viewers; they actively participate in trends, challenges, and viral content.** The platform's interactive features, such as duets and stitching, encourage users to create their own versions of popular videos, thereby amplifying content reach and fostering community involvement. This participatory culture presents a unique opportunity for brands to engage with users in creative and meaningful ways. By launching challenges or leveraging trending hashtags, brands can inspire user-generated content that promotes their products or services organically.

TikTok's global reach and diverse user base also contribute to its distinctive appeal. While the platform is immensely popular in the United States, it has a significant presence in other markets, including Europe, Asia, and Latin America. This international audience brings together a wide range of cultures, languages, and interests, allowing brands to tailor their marketing strategies to different regions and demographics. The ability to connect with a global audience through localized content makes TikTok an invaluable tool for brands looking to expand their reach and influence.

Moreover, **TikTok's algorithm is designed to surface content that resonates with individual users, based on their viewing habits and interactions.** This personalized approach ensures that users are constantly exposed to content that aligns with their interests, increasing the likelihood of engagement. For marketers, this means that high-quality, relevant content has the potential to go viral, even if the creator has a relatively small following. By focusing on creating engaging and shareable content, brands can capitalize on TikTok's algorithm to enhance their visibility and impact.

CREATING ENGAGING TIKTOK CONTENT

Creating engaging content on TikTok requires a blend of creativity, authenticity, and a keen understanding of the platform's unique features. Unlike other social media platforms, TikTok thrives on short, impactful videos that capture attention quickly and inspire interaction. Here are some pro tips and tricks to help you create content that resonates with the TikTok audience and drives engagement.

1. Understand Your Audience and Trends
To create content that resonates, it's crucial to understand your audience and the trends that captivate them. Spend time exploring TikTok to see what types of content are trending and how users are engaging with it. Follow popular creators and hashtags in your niche to stay updated on current trends and challenges. TikTok's "For You" page is a valuable resource for discovering trending content and getting inspiration for your own videos.

2. Capture Attention Quickly
TikTok users scroll through content rapidly, so it's essential to capture their attention within the first few seconds of your video. Start with a strong hook that immediately grabs attention, whether it's a surprising statement, a visually striking scene, or an intriguing question. Keep your content concise and to the point, as the platform favors shorter videos that deliver value quickly.

3. Leverage Popular Music and Sounds

Music is a core element of TikTok's appeal. Using trending songs or sounds can make your content more discoverable and relatable. Explore TikTok's library of music and sounds to find those that complement your content. When you use popular audio, your video has a higher chance of appearing in search results and on the "For You" page. Make sure to align the music with the mood and message of your video to enhance its impact.

4. Embrace Creativity and Authenticity

TikTok values creativity and authenticity over polished perfection. Users appreciate content that feels genuine and relatable. Don't be afraid to experiment with different styles and formats to find what works best for you. Use humor, storytelling, and personal anecdotes to create a connection with your audience. Authenticity builds trust and encourages viewers to engage with your content.

5. Participate in Challenges and Trends

Participating in challenges and trends is a great way to increase your visibility on TikTok. Keep an eye on popular hashtags and challenges, and create your own version of trending content. Adding your unique twist can make your videos stand out. Challenges often have built-in audiences searching for related content, which can boost your video's reach and engagement.

6. Use Captions and Text Overlays

Adding captions and text overlays can enhance the accessibility and engagement of your videos. Captions help convey your message to viewers who watch with the sound off and can highlight key points or calls-to-action. Use text overlays to provide context, emphasize important information, or add humor. Ensure the text is clear, readable, and complements the visual content.

7. Optimize Your Hashtags and Descriptions

Effective use of hashtags and descriptions can improve the discoverability of your content. Use a mix of popular, niche-specific, and branded hashtags to reach a broader audience. Your video description should be concise and include relevant keywords and hashtags. Engaging descriptions can also encourage viewers to interact with your content by asking questions or prompting comments.

8. Engage with Your Audience

Building a community on TikTok requires active engagement with your audience. Respond to comments, ask questions, and encourage viewers to share their thoughts. Engaging with your audience fosters a sense of community and loyalty. You can also collaborate with other creators or respond to their content using TikTok's duet and stitch features, which can introduce your channel to new viewers.

9. Utilize TikTok's Editing Tools and Effects

TikTok offers a variety of built-in editing tools and effects to enhance your videos. Experiment with filters, transitions, and effects to make your content more visually appealing and dynamic. Use the green screen effect to create interesting backgrounds or the time-lapse feature to speed up your videos. Mastering these tools can help you produce professional-looking content that stands out.

10. Post Consistently and Analyze Performance

Consistency is key to growing your presence on TikTok. Develop a regular posting schedule to keep your audience engaged and attract new followers. Pay attention to your video analytics to understand what types of content perform best. Metrics such as views, likes, shares, and comments provide insights into your audience's preferences and behaviors. Use this data to refine your content strategy and improve future videos.

LEVERAGING TRENDS AND CHALLENGES

TikTok's dynamic and fast-paced environment thrives on trends and challenges that can propel content into virality. Leveraging these trends and challenges is crucial for maximizing your reach and engagement on the platform. By staying current with what's popular and creatively participating in these movements, you can significantly enhance your TikTok marketing strategy.

1. Understanding the Power of Trends and Challenges

Trends and challenges on TikTok often emerge from user creativity, pop culture, and current events. They can range from specific dance routines and song lip-syncs to hashtag-driven themes and viral memes. Participating in these trends allows brands to tap into an existing wave of engagement, making their content more discoverable and relatable. By aligning your content with these popular movements, you can boost visibility, attract new followers, and foster a sense of community.

2. Identifying Current Trends and Challenges

To effectively leverage trends and challenges, it's essential to stay updated with what's happening on the platform. Explore TikTok's "Discover" page regularly to see trending hashtags, sounds, and popular challenges. Follow influential creators and keep an eye on what's gaining traction in your niche.

Popular Trends in 2024:

a. Eco-Challenges: With the increasing focus on sustainability, eco-friendly challenges have gained immense popularity. These challenges encourage users to showcase their efforts in reducing waste, recycling, and promoting green living.

b. AI-Generated Art: Leveraging advancements in AI, users are creating and sharing AI-generated artwork and animations. This trend has sparked a wave of creativity, with creators experimenting with AI tools to produce unique content.

c. Retro Rewinds: Nostalgia continues to be a powerful trend, with users revisiting the '80s, '90s, and early 2000s. This involves fashion throwbacks, retro music lip-syncs, and recreating old TV show scenes or commercials.

d. Health and Wellness Challenges: Challenges promoting mental and physical health have become increasingly popular. From daily workout routines and mindfulness practices to healthy eating tips, these challenges encourage users to share their wellness journeys.

3. Creating Content that Rides the Trend Wave

a. Authentic Participation:
When participating in trends and challenges, ensure your content feels authentic and aligns with your brand values. Forced or irrelevant participation can be off-putting to viewers. Instead, find creative ways to integrate the trend with your brand message.

b. Adding a Unique Twist:
While it's important to follow the trend's basic format, adding your unique twist can make your content stand out. This could be through humor, special effects, or incorporating your products or services in an innovative way.

c. Collaborating with Influencers:
Partnering with popular TikTok influencers who are already engaging with trends can amplify your reach. Influencers can bring credibility and introduce your brand to their established audience, increasing your content's impact.

4. Best Practices for Leveraging Trends and Challenges

a. Quick Execution:
- Trends on TikTok move fast. To capitalize on a trend, it's crucial to act quickly. The sooner you create and post your content after identifying a trend, the higher the chances of your video gaining traction.

b. Quality and Creativity:
While speed is essential, quality should not be compromised. Ensure your videos are well-produced and creatively executed. High-quality visuals, engaging narratives, and clear audio can significantly enhance viewer experience.

c. Use Relevant Hashtags:
Hashtags are vital for making your content discoverable. Use trending hashtags relevant to the challenge or trend you're participating in. This increases the likelihood of your video appearing in search results and on the "For You" page.

d. Engage with the Community:
Engage with other users participating in the same trend or challenge. Like, comment, and share their content to build relationships and increase the visibility of your own content. Community engagement can foster a supportive environment that boosts your presence.

5. Measuring Success and Adapting

a. Analyze Performance:
Use TikTok Analytics to track the performance of your trend-related content. Monitor metrics such as views, likes, shares, and comments to gauge the effectiveness of your participation.

b. Learn and Adapt:
Not all trends will work equally well for your brand. Analyze which trends brought the most engagement and why. Use these insights to refine your approach for future trends and challenges.

ADVERTISING ON TIKTOK

Advertising on TikTok offers brands a powerful way to reach a highly engaged and diverse audience. The platform's unique format and interactive features make it an ideal space for creative and impactful advertising.

1. Types of TikTok Ads and Suitable Content

a. In-Feed Ads:

These are short video ads that appear in users' "For You" feed, blending seamlessly with organic content.

Content Tips: Create engaging, high-quality videos that capture attention within the first few seconds. Use compelling visuals, clear messaging, and a strong call-to-action (CTA). Interactive elements like polls or challenges can enhance engagement.

b. Branded Hashtag Challenges:

These ads invite users to participate in a challenge using a specific hashtag created by your brand.

Content Tips: Develop a fun and easy-to-join challenge that aligns with your brand. Use influencers to kickstart the challenge and provide clear instructions to encourage participation. Highlight user-generated content to build community and authenticity.

c. Branded Effects:

Custom AR filters, stickers, and effects that users can apply to their own videos.

Content Tips: Design creative and appealing effects that resonate with your audience. Ensure the effects are easy to use and fun, encouraging widespread adoption and sharing. Integrate subtle brand elements to enhance recognition without being intrusive.

d. TopView Ads:

These are full-screen ads that appear when users first open the TikTok app, ensuring maximum visibility.

Content Tips: Make a strong first impression with visually stunning and engaging content. Keep the message clear and impactful, with a focus on brand awareness. Utilize bold visuals, dynamic transitions, and memorable music.

e. Spark Ads:

This format allows brands to boost their own organic content or user-generated content that mentions their brand.

Content Tips: Identify high-performing organic content and use Spark Ads to amplify its reach. Choose content that naturally resonates with your audience and aligns with your brand values. Leverage authentic user testimonials and creative user-generated videos.

2. Budget Considerations

a. Setting a Budget:

TikTok offers flexible budgeting options to accommodate various campaign sizes. You can set daily or total budgets based on your advertising goals and available resources.

Start with a test budget to understand what works best for your brand and audience. Adjust your spending based on the performance and insights gathered from initial campaigns.

b. Cost Structures:

CPM (Cost Per Mille): Pay per thousand impressions. Suitable for brand awareness campaigns aiming for maximum reach.

CPC (Cost Per Click): Pay per click on your ad. Ideal for campaigns focused on driving traffic to a website or landing page.

CPV (Cost Per View): Pay per video view. Useful for video content where engagement and view duration are critical.

c. Minimum Spend:

TikTok generally requires a minimum campaign spend, which can vary based on the ad format and targeting options. Consult TikTok's advertising guidelines or your account manager for specific details.

3. Targeting Strategies

a. Demographic Targeting:

Age, Gender, and Location: Tailor your ads to specific demographic groups to ensure relevance. For example, target younger users for trendy fashion items or older demographics for financial services.

b. Interest Targeting:

Target users based on their interests and behaviors on TikTok. This can include categories like gaming, beauty, fitness, travel, and more. Utilize TikTok's data to align your ads with users' preferences.

c. Custom Audiences:

First-Party Data: Upload your own customer lists to create custom audiences. This is effective for retargeting existing customers or reaching similar profiles.

Engagement-Based: Create audiences based on engagement with your previous content, such as video views, profile visits, or ad interactions.

d. Lookalike Audiences:

Use lookalike audiences to reach users similar to your existing customers or high-engagement followers. This expands your reach to potential new customers who share similar characteristics.

e. Behavioral Targeting:

Target users based on their interactions with content on TikTok, such as video views, likes, shares, and comments. This ensures your ads reach an engaged and relevant audience.

4. Best Practices for TikTok Advertising

a. Emphasize Authenticity:

Create ads that feel native to TikTok's environment. Avoid overly polished, corporate-style videos. Instead, focus on authenticity, creativity, and relatability.

b. Test and Optimize:

Continuously test different ad formats, creatives, and targeting options. Use A/B testing to compare performance and optimize your campaigns based on data-driven insights.

c. Leverage Influencers:

Collaborate with TikTok influencers to amplify your reach and credibility. Choose influencers whose audience aligns with your target market and whose content style matches your brand.

d. Engage with Trends:

Participate in trending challenges and use popular music to increase your ad's relevance and visibility. Aligning your content with current trends can boost engagement and viewership.

e. Monitor Performance:

Use TikTok's analytics tools to track key performance metrics such as impressions, clicks, conversions, and engagement rates. Regularly review these metrics to understand the effectiveness of your ads and make necessary adjustments.

CHAPTER 8

Integrating Content and Video Marketing

CREATING A COHESIVE STRATEGY

Integrating content and video marketing into a cohesive strategy is essential for maximizing the impact of your marketing efforts. A well-rounded strategy ensures that your content and video initiatives complement each other, delivering a consistent message across all channels and engaging your audience effectively.

1. Define Clear Objectives

The first step in creating a cohesive content and video marketing strategy is to define clear, measurable objectives. Your goals should align with your overall business objectives and provide direction for your marketing efforts. Common objectives include:

- **Brand Awareness:** Increase visibility and recognition of your brand.
- **Lead Generation:** Attract potential customers and gather their contact information.
- **Customer Engagement:** Foster interactions and build relationships with your audience.
- **Sales and Conversions:** Drive purchases or other desired actions.

Clearly defined objectives will guide your content creation and distribution efforts, ensuring that each piece of content and video serves a specific purpose.

2. Understand Your Audience

To create content and videos that resonate with your audience, you need to understand their preferences, behaviors, and needs. Develop detailed buyer personas that represent your ideal customers, including demographic information, interests, pain points, and preferred content formats. Use surveys, social media insights, and analytics tools to gather data and refine your personas.

Understanding your audience will help you tailor your content and videos to address their specific needs and preferences, making your marketing efforts more effective. Don't post 10 reels a week on Instagram because that's what other do. Listen to your target audience more than your non-target audience.

3. Develop a Content Plan

A comprehensive content plan outlines the types of content and videos you will create, the topics you will cover, and the schedule for publishing. Your content plan should include:

- **Content Types:** Blog posts, social media updates, infographics, case studies, e-books, webinars, podcasts, etc.
- **Video Types:** Explainer videos, product demos, tutorials, customer testimonials, live streams, behind-the-scenes videos, etc.
- **Topics and Themes:** Key themes and topics that align with your audience's interests and your brand's expertise.
- **Publishing Schedule:** A calendar that outlines when and where each piece of content and video will be published.

By planning your content and videos in advance, you can ensure a consistent flow of high-quality material that keeps your audience engaged.

4. Ensure Consistent Branding and Messaging

Consistency is crucial for building brand recognition and trust. Ensure that all your content and videos adhere to your brand guidelines, including visual elements, tone of voice, and messaging. Use consistent branding elements such as logos, colors, and fonts across all platforms.

Your messaging should reinforce your brand's value proposition and key messages. Whether it's a blog post, a social media update, or a video, each piece of content should contribute to a cohesive brand narrative.

5. Optimize for Each Platform

Different platforms have unique characteristics and audiences, so it's important to tailor your content and videos accordingly. Optimize your content for each platform to maximize its impact:

- **Website and Blog:** Focus on SEO-friendly long-form content that provides in-depth information and value.
- **YouTube:** Create engaging, high-quality videos with compelling thumbnails and optimized titles, descriptions, and tags.
- **Social Media:** Develop short, attention-grabbing content that encourages interaction and sharing. Use platform-specific features such as Instagram Stories, Facebook Live, and LinkedIn articles.
- **Email Marketing:** Craft personalized and relevant content that drives engagement and conversions. Incorporate videos to enhance the email experience.

By optimizing your content for each platform, you can ensure that it reaches the right audience and achieves the desired outcomes.

6. Promote Cross-Channel Integration

Integrating your content and video marketing efforts across multiple channels amplifies their reach and impact. Promote your videos through blog posts, social media updates, and email newsletters. Embed videos on your website and landing pages to increase engagement and dwell time.

Cross-channel integration also involves repurposing content to extend its lifespan. For example, you can turn a blog post into a video, create an infographic from a webinar, or share snippets of a video on social media.

7. Measure and Analyze Performance

To ensure that your content and video marketing strategy is effective, you need to measure and analyze its performance regularly. Use analytics tools to track key metrics such as:

- **Engagement:** Likes, shares, comments, and views.
- **Traffic:** Website visits, referral sources, and bounce rates.
- Conversions: Leads generated, sales, and other desired actions.
- Retention: Audience retention rates and repeat engagement.

Analyzing these metrics will provide insights into what works and what doesn't, allowing you to refine your strategy and improve future efforts.

8. Continuously Optimize and Improve

Marketing is an iterative process, and continuous optimization is key to long-term success. Based on your performance analysis, make data-driven adjustments to your content and video strategy. Experiment with different formats, topics, and distribution channels to find what resonates best with your audience.

Regularly update and refresh your content to keep it relevant and engaging. Stay informed about industry trends and emerging platforms to adapt your strategy accordingly.

REPURPOSING CONTENT ACROSS DIFFERENT FORMATS

Repurposing content is a strategic approach to maximize the value of your content by adapting it to various formats and platforms. This not only extends the lifespan of your content but also ensures it reaches a broader audience through their preferred channels. Repurposing content effectively can enhance your content marketing strategy, improve SEO, and drive more engagement.

1. Understanding the Benefits of Content Repurposing

Repurposing content offers several benefits that can significantly enhance your marketing efforts:

Extended Reach: Different audiences prefer different content formats. By repurposing content, you can reach a wider audience across various platforms.

Increased ROI: Maximizing the use of existing content reduces the time and resources needed to create new content, thereby increasing your return on investment.

Improved SEO: Multiple formats of the same content can increase your presence across search engines, driving more traffic to your website.

Consistent Messaging: Repurposing ensures a consistent message across all channels, reinforcing your brand's value proposition.

2. Identifying Content Suitable for Repurposing

Not all content is equally suitable for repurposing. Identify high-performing content that resonates with your audience and addresses their needs. Content that provides valuable insights, evergreen topics, and detailed guides or tutorials are ideal candidates for repurposing.

3. Practical Examples of Content Repurposing

a. Blog Posts to Videos:

Transform detailed blog posts into engaging videos by summarizing key points, adding visuals, and including a voiceover or on-screen text.

- Example: Convert a "How-to" blog post into a step-by-step tutorial video and upload it to YouTube, embed it on your website, and share snippets on social media.

b. Webinars to E-books:

Compile the information presented in a webinar into a comprehensive e-book. Include additional insights, case studies, and visual elements like charts and infographics.

- Example: If you hosted a webinar on "Digital Marketing Strategies," turn it into an e-book titled "The Ultimate Guide to Digital Marketing Strategies," available for download on your website.

c. Infographics to Blog Posts:

Expand the data and points presented in an infographic into a detailed blog post. Provide context, explanations, and additional resources.

- Example: Take an infographic on "Social Media Statistics" and write a blog post elaborating on each statistic, its implications, and how businesses can leverage these insights.

d. Podcasts to Articles:

Transcribe podcast episodes and edit them into readable articles. Highlight key takeaways, quotes, and actionable advice.

- Example: If you have a podcast episode discussing "Content Marketing Trends," turn it into an article summarizing the main trends discussed, with time-stamped quotes for reference.

e. Case Studies to Social Media Posts:

Break down detailed case studies into bite-sized social media posts. Highlight the problem, solution, and results in a series of posts.

- Example: Create a series of LinkedIn posts from a case study on a successful client project, each post focusing on a different aspect of the case study.

4. Best Practices for Content Repurposing

a. Tailor Content for Each Platform:

Adapt the format and style of the repurposed content to suit the specific platform. For instance, a video created from a blog post might need a different approach for YouTube compared to Instagram.

b. Maintain Consistency in Branding:

Ensure that repurposed content maintains consistent branding, including visual elements, tone of voice, and messaging. This helps reinforce brand recognition and trust.

c. Update and Refresh Content:

When repurposing older content, update it with the latest information, statistics, and examples to keep it relevant and valuable to your audience.

d. Cross-Promote Content:

Promote repurposed content across all your channels. For example, share a blog post on your social media, include the video in your email newsletter, and link the e-book in your YouTube video description.

e. Measure Performance and Adjust:

Track the performance of repurposed content using analytics tools. Monitor metrics such as engagement, reach, and conversions to understand what works best and make necessary adjustments.

CASE STUDIES OF SUCCESSFUL CONTENT AND VIDEO MARKETING CAMPAIGNS

Examining real-world examples of successful content and video marketing campaigns can provide valuable insights and inspiration for your own strategies. These case studies showcase how different brands have effectively integrated content and video marketing to achieve their goals, offering practical lessons on what works in the digital marketing landscape.

1. Nike: "You Can't Stop Us" Campaign

In 2020, Nike launched the "You Can't Stop Us" campaign, a powerful video marketing initiative aimed at promoting unity and resilience during the global COVID-19 pandemic. The campaign featured a split-screen video highlighting athletes and individuals from diverse backgrounds overcoming challenges and continuing their passions despite the pandemic.

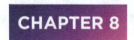
Integrating Content & Video Marketing

Strategy:

Video Production: The video was masterfully edited to show seamless transitions between athletes, emphasizing unity and collective strength. It featured both well-known athletes and everyday people.

Content Distribution: Nike shared the video across multiple platforms, including YouTube, Instagram, Twitter, and Facebook, ensuring maximum reach.

Emotional Appeal: The campaign leveraged strong emotional storytelling to connect with viewers on a personal level, fostering a sense of hope and resilience.

Results:

The video quickly went viral, amassing millions of views across platforms.

It generated extensive media coverage and positive public response.

Nike reinforced its brand image as a supporter of both professional athletes and everyday individuals, aligning with its core values of inspiration and innovation.

Lessons Learned:

Emotional storytelling and high-quality production can significantly enhance engagement.

Consistent messaging across multiple platforms ensures broader reach and impact.

Addressing current events and societal issues can make campaigns more relevant and resonant.

2. Blendtec: "Will It Blend?" Series

Blendtec, a blender manufacturer, launched the "Will It Blend?" video series, where founder Tom Dickson blended various unconventional items (like iPhones, marbles, and golf balls) to showcase the power and durability of Blendtec blenders. This creative and entertaining approach turned Blendtec into a viral sensation.

Strategy:

Content Innovation: Blendtec focused on creating unique and entertaining content that highlighted their product's capabilities in a memorable way.

Consistency: The videos were released regularly, creating anticipation and keeping the audience engaged.

SEO and Social Sharing: The videos were optimized for search engines and heavily promoted on YouTube and social media, making them easily discoverable and shareable.

Results:

The series attracted millions of views on YouTube and significantly boosted brand visibility.

Sales of Blendtec blenders increased by 700%, demonstrating the direct impact of the campaign on revenue.

The campaign earned media coverage and a strong online presence, establishing Blendtec as an innovative and fun brand.

Lessons Learned:
Creative and entertaining content can capture attention and drive engagement.

Consistency in content creation helps build and maintain an audience.

Viral marketing can significantly boost brand awareness and sales.

3. Red Bull: Stratos Jump

Red Bull's Stratos Jump is one of the most iconic examples of content and video marketing. In 2012, Red Bull sponsored skydiver Felix Baumgartner's record-breaking jump from the stratosphere, which was streamed live and documented in a series of videos.

Strategy:
High-Stakes Event: The campaign centered around a high-stakes, record-breaking event that captivated global audiences.

Live Streaming and Documentation: Red Bull leveraged live streaming to capture real-time audience engagement and followed up with detailed video content documenting the event.

Cross-Platform Promotion: The campaign was promoted across multiple channels, including YouTube, social media, and traditional media, ensuring extensive reach.

Results:

The live stream attracted over 9.5 million viewers, setting a record for the most-watched live event on YouTube at the time.

Red Bull's brand visibility and association with extreme sports and adventure were significantly enhanced.

The campaign generated massive media coverage and long-term engagement through follow-up content.

Lessons Learned:

High-profile events can generate substantial buzz and engagement.

Live streaming combined with detailed documentation maximizes both real-time and ongoing audience interest.

Cross-platform promotion ensures broad and sustained reach.

4. HubSpot: Inbound Marketing Content Strategy

HubSpot, a leader in inbound marketing and sales software, has effectively used content marketing to attract, engage, and convert leads. Their comprehensive content strategy includes blogs, e-books, webinars, videos, and social media content aimed at educating their audience on inbound marketing practices.

Integrating Content & Video Marketing

Strategy:

<u>Educational Content:</u> HubSpot focuses on creating high-quality educational content that addresses the needs and pain points of their target audience.

<u>SEO Optimization:</u> Their content is optimized for search engines, ensuring high visibility and organic traffic.

<u>Lead Generation:</u> HubSpot offers valuable resources like e-books and webinars in exchange for contact information, effectively generating leads.

Results:

HubSpot's blog attracts millions of visitors monthly, driving significant traffic to their website.

Their educational content has positioned HubSpot as an authority in inbound marketing.

The lead generation strategy has contributed to sustained business growth and customer acquisition.

Lessons Learned:

Educational content that addresses audience needs can drive traffic and establish authority.

SEO optimization is crucial for content visibility and organic growth.

Offering valuable resources in exchange for contact information is an effective lead generation tactic.

www.ingramcontent.com/pod-product-compliance
Lightning Source LLC
La Vergne TN
LVHW051641050326
832903LV00022B/840